CONFRONTING FASCISM

Discussion Documents
for a Militant Movement

Don Hamerquist

J. Sakai

Anti-Racist Action Chicago

Mark Salotte

KER
SPL
EBE
DEB
2017

Confronting Fascism:
Discussion Documents for a Militant Movement
ISBN 978-1-894946-87-2

Second edition Kersplebedeb 2017
first printing

Kersplebedeb Publishing and Distribution
CP 63560
CCCP Van Horne
Montreal, Quebec
Canada H3W 3H8
email: info@kersplebedeb.com
web: www.kersplebedeb.com
         www.leftwingbooks.net

TABLE OF CONTENTS

PREFACE

Fascism, understanding it and how we combat it, is as important today as when we first put this book together fifteen years ago. Mass protests against the new U.S. administration often have an explicit anti-fascism to them. This is an important shift, as previous antifa struggles were generally against specific Nazi groups like the KKK, National Alliance, and World Church of the Creator. Militant campaigns by Anti-Racist Action put serious pressures on the old fascist groupings making it difficult for them to organize. Without overstating the role of the radical antifascist movement, the reality is that by the mid-2000s most of the established Nazi organizations had ceased to function in any real way.

In this moment, fascist potentialities emerge in the context of the rise of Right populisms. They are largely white and racialist, often virulently anti-immigrant and anti-Muslim, combining social and economic anxiety about (and sometimes a clear rejection of) the costs of decades of neoliberal globalization, war and expansion of capitalist Empire. The recent election cycle and new administration puts this on full display.

However, while we see more aggressive policies from the State level we are also seeing racist and fascist attacks from non-State actors: the massacre at

Mother Emmanuel in Charleston, SC; the shootings in North Minneapolis of people engaged in protests against the police murder of Jamar Clark; attacks on Mosques in Texas and Quebec City where worshipers were shot dead; the shooting of an IWW member by an Alt Right supporter in Seattle. It was not the State carrying out these attacks but instead people inspired by racialist, anti-immigrant and sometimes explicitly fascist ideas. The Charleston shooter was an avid supporter of Nazi and Confederate ideology, the Minneapolis 4th Precinct shooters were inspired by far-right and fascist militias. These were planned attacks on Black people and symbols of the Black freedom movements. Clearly white fascist push back.

Globally there is deepening crisis and uncertainty. War and repression with millions dead and displaced have led to mass immigration, which in turn has been exploited by Far-Right anti-immigrant/anti-refugee movements with open links to fascists. In the war zones there are non-liberatory insurgencies drawing in the dominant States. Simultaneously the U.S and Russia claim their interventions are some form of "antifascism."

In Eastern Europe fascism and antifascism are even more tangled. War in Ukraine has divided our movements, with antifa fighting on all sides and at times against each other. Against Russian imperialist maneuvers intending to seize Ukrainian territory, Ukrainian Far-Right nationalists call for the common defense of all Ukrainians regardless of race and religion. While Russian-backed leaderships in the eastern Peoples Republics recruit National Socialists to prosecute the war, destabilizing the region with a strategy to transform the east into a Novorossiya. With an "antifascism" incorporating Soviet nostalgia, the Russian-backed enclaves get support from anti-NATO coalitions comprised of Stalinists, anti-imperialists, Far-Right political parties and Nazis.

It would seem fascism and antifascism are not any clearer today than they were when we first went to press. However there is more demand for this book now than at any point previously. It's becoming part of the recommended readings for those trying to think more critically. The result is that ideas (and lessons) in here have been taken up, debated and applied when possible.

Some Locals of the IWW's General Defense Committee combine class struggle and militant antifascism into a broader notion of community self-defense. TORCH Antifa Network, independent Antifa and ARA groups have attempted to develop working strategies heavily indebted to concerns raised in this book.

Three Way Fight started as an online extension of *Confronting Fascism* connecting it to antifascist and revolutionary anti-capitalist struggles. Matthew Lyons's research and regular contributions to the site has made an invaluable contribution to the development of a revolutionary anti-fascism.

And importantly, Kersplebedeb has kept the book alive, now with this second edition.

All of these projects and movements have helped deepen our efforts at confronting both fascism and the dominant authoritarian and capitalist system. In doing so we continue to locate, uncover and build upon the necessary elements that are part of building a popular revolutionary and liberatory alternative. It's time to be out in the mix.

Xtn
February 2017

ARA

SHUTDOWN THE KLAN

INTRODUCTION

Xtn of Anti-Racist Action Chicago

For North American radicals the change of the century was marked not by New Year's Eve celebrations but in fireworks of a totally different kind — N30 (Nov. 30, 1999, in Seattle) and 9/11 (Sept. 11, 2001, in D.C. and New York). The first opened up an entire range of new and energizing possibilities. It heralded in an era of mass street protest unseen by most of us. It exposed the weakness of capitalist power and hegemony and was enough to make us feel that anything was possible. The second brought entirely new elements into the picture. We were not the only enemy of the capitalist order, and this new enemy was no friend of liberation. Post-Seattle, the new street protest movement developed and even accelerated at a pace that politicized thousands — but there were growing problems. With 9/11 the Seattle spirit melted into confusion and disarray.

Out of this energy and confusion comes this little book. It's an attempt to look at this new era of political action and thought, focusing on an area that we see as extremely important, relevant and perhaps at the core to what's in the air today — fascism. You are holding in your hands our attempt to begin a different and more serious discussion of fascism, what is it, of the relationship of fascism to capitalism, and of the elements of a strategy with the potential to defeat both. The essays presented here should be taken as part of an ongoing, evolving talk within the movement—with the emphasis on "ongoing." Unlike many publications and political statements that try to be the authoritative "final word" on the subject, the documents here are meant to raise more questions than they necessarily answer. They're about jump-starting our minds and removing any blinders, allowing us to see things as we haven't seen them before.

For us, the most important aspect of these essays is that they take fascism seriously as a force/ideology/movement/tendency. They point out that fascism isn't just connected to dusty history books in the back of the university library but that it is present in some of the most important events in political history, both in the past and in what's going on today.

The actual genesis of these essays lies in the period right before N30. Anti-fascist activity was heating up in the U.S. Midwest, directed primarily against the neo-nazi organization called the World Church of Creator (WCOTC). As the actions intensified, questions started emerging — as did differences. A Chicago, Illinois, chapter of Anti-Racist Action (ARA) had initiated a campaign to shut down a series of public meetings planned by WCOTC leader Matt Hale. The campaign started by ARA eventually made it difficult and even impossible for Hale and his organization to rally, let alone go out in public, without a challenge — politically as well as physically.

During this time, the Battle of Seattle grabbed everyone's attention and made us sit up. Images of thousands of protesters clogging the streets of downtown Seattle were broadcast on every television across the world — so too were scenes of the

Black Bloc and the attacks on capitalist property and police. Newspapers were scrambling for info on the new street militants and their ideology of anarchism. And debate started to rage in the radical press. The Black Bloc was seen by some as wrong-headed youth interested only in adventurism. Sometimes the Black Bloc was condemned outright and treated as criminal—an attitude that rolled in from the established Left. During the riots, liberal and leftist do-gooders actually tried to defend capitalist property from the anarchists. In several instances, avowed "pacifists" attacked the Black Bloc in an effort to protect places like the Gap and Starbucks.

The actions by the Black Bloc and anarchists turned traditional politics on its head. This black-clad voice in the protest movement wasn't content to beg the politicians and capitalists for reforms. The Black Bloc symbolized a new generation of activists wanting nothing short of revolution.

The ranks of the Black Bloc were comprised of many activists who had actually cut their teeth fighting nazis and Klan groups. ARA groups quickly defended the Seattle Black Bloc, seeing a similarity in tactics and motivation—and also in the way that militant antifascism had suffered from denunciations by the established left and liberal reformists. It was important for us to acknowledge and embrace this break with past thinking and action. But ARA activists were also becoming aware of other tendencies riding on the waves of the protests.

"Anti-globalization" was an amorphous concept that was defined at its lowest denominator as a mass challenge to the control and influence of international corporations. This movement was a political free-for-all that gave room to a wide range of ideological tendencies from left to right—including fascists. As the Seattle streets were lighting up in the flames of protest, just an hour to the north Matt Hale was visiting Washington State to participate in a remembrance ceremony for Robert Matthews, the slain leader of the neo-nazi paramilitary organization, the Order. Hale praised the demonstrations in Seattle and in particular hailed the young rioters as heroes. He chastised the right-wing establishment for being do-nothings and reformist and said that the fascist movement could take lessons from the militant tactics of the demonstrators and Black Bloc. The anti-fascist and anarchist movement now saw that this anti-globalization movement was not a single homogenous block. It was not only the reformist left and its ultimate subservience to the state that had to be challenged—the racist and fascist elements that would continue to insert themselves into the mix had to be exposed and beat back.

From N30 onward, global protest politics were characterized by a willingness to fight back and break the law. Even more passive, non-violent demonstrators showed an unprecedented determination in disrupting the capitalist machine. Everywhere, from the big cities to little country towns, radical anti-capitalist and anarchist actions, graffiti and groups started to emerge. For those who couldn't be in Seattle, the next big demo was prioritized. The spirit of revolt was catching everyone.

This vibe of uncompromising protest, and the awareness of a growing and vocal nazi movement, only helped to encourage anti-fascist organizing. The WCOTC, one of the fastest growing and most dynamic of nazi groups, was facing opposition everywhere it tried to rally. From Indiana to New England to Hale's hometown of Peoria, Illinois, antifa were throwing up resistance. (One time, sitting at a bar, a bunch of Midwestern antifa looked up to see hand-to-hand streetfighting between anarchist anti-racists and nazis after a WCOTC rally in Wallingford, Connecticut, courtesy of CNN.) But the increase in activity — both anti-fascist and anti-capitalist — didn't come without growing problems. An increase in state surveillance and repression coincided with the growth of the new movement. Antifa also faced the always-present risk of fascist counter-attacks.

At the same time, various radicals started asking whether anti-fascist organizing should be a priority for placing our energies. What was to be gained by doing anti-fascist work? Do groups like the ARA see more of a threat in nazis than what really exists? These questions demanded answers, which helped antifa to clarify our motivations and positions and

provided us with a platform to argue out why we do what we do.

Hamerquist's essay was a direct response to these questions. In it he makes a strong case for why anti-fascist organizing is an essential component to the development of a genuine liberation movement. Originally shorter, the essay focused on several key points: organization and cadre building; questions of violence and challenging reformist tendencies in the movement (both antifa and revolutionary); developing a critique of the Left's historical analysis and assumptions of fascism; and looking at new, potentially anti-capitalist tendencies that may emerge from within a popular and revolutionary fascism.

As Hamerquist's essay started to circulate among a small network of anti-fascists and anarchists, it was proposed to turn it into a pamphlet and distribute it to a wider audience. Sakai, author of an essay on right-wing tendencies in the anti-globalization movement, was approached to write an introduction and critique of what Hamerquist laid out. Sakai soon discarded his initial draft when another event rocked our world—the attacks that sent the World Trade Center and part of the Pentagon up in flames.

9/11 had a profound effect on the political climate and quickly sent the new era of dissent and protest into disarray. Some within the anti-globalization and anti-capitalist movement attempted to maintain the energy of the previous two years, but overall the movement here in the U.S. was sapped of its potency. After a while, even the anti-war momentum came to a standstill. Today, there is still bombing in Afghanistan killing hundreds. Where's the anti-war activity? Where's the outrage? 9/11 was the biggest silencer of the growing anti-capitalist movement that the capitalists could have prayed for. Why is that?

The anti-fascist movement also had to deal with this new climate. Pre-9/11, antifa had continued to merge into the anti-globalization movement, with many participating in the quickly emerging—and explicitly revolutionary—anti-capitalist wing, often taking leading roles in planning and actions. From the protests against the Trans-Atlantic Business Dialogue in Cincinnati, Ohio, to the Black Bloc at the A16 anti-IMF/World Bank meeting in D.C., hundreds of antifa and ARA activists joined in and became a visible presence. The radical anti-racist voice these activists brought had previously been non-existent in any noticeable organized expression. This trend continued into the Quebec City anti-FTAA actions and was also massively present when European antifa marched in Prague and Gottenburg. Antifa worldwide became important players in the new movement, organizing as a block against reactionary politics and fascist attempts to join the protests. But once the airliners-turned-cruise missiles blasted their way into global consciousness, anti-fascists and revolutionaries had to deal with the rapidly changing landscape. We could not ignore the unfolding war, roundups and political repression, but we were not ready for them.

Anti-fascists attempted to analyze the attacks and who may have perpetrated them. Articles informed the movement of both the nature of fascist entities like the Taliban and what the Western capitalist response to them and similar movements would be.

Antifa also took note of fascist and neo-nazi views on 9/11 and its effect. Many of the U.S. fascist groups were strategizing on how to take advantage of the mass hysteria that immediately sprang up and were looking to use the loss of security that was present as a way to insert themselves into the picture. In an immediate climate that had mobs of people attacking Arabs, Asians and other people of color perceived as "outsiders" to America, the fascists worked to promote these hostilities and fears. The immediate after-effects of 9/11 were very, very ugly. Those who tried to speak out against the war and the rampant racism were beat up and threatened. Mosques were burned down, gas attendants were attacked with machetes and businesses were shot up. All hell seemed to have broken loose. And the fascist movement now had a perfect opportunity to build itself.

This takes us back to this little publication. In these essays, the authors both discuss the dynamics of fascism and the potentially revolutionary impulses behind it. Fascism is no friend of humanity, and when they call fascism "revolutionary" they don't mean "progressive" or "liberatory." Fascism has a revolutionary component because it is about a complete re-shaping of modern society, transforming how we look and deal with one another, who has power and who doesn't and who's going to get ethnically cleansed. The essays also point out that fascism will be based in mass support—it has to be. Fascism is not a room full of capitalist bosses or lackeys saying, "Ok, we're gonna institute fascism now." No, fascism is a movement made up of lots and lots of disgruntled people. And if we are to be successful in fighting fascism, then this is where we have to begin.

Our strategy must be about popularizing our ideas and engaging in struggles that open up conflict with state and capitalist interests. We need to see where the political fissures exist and figure out how to intervene in ways that crack them open even further. But what is our strategy? And what are the politics and ideas that provide the basis for our approach?

Fascism gains ground when a popular upsurge of people decide it's time for a change and head down the path that leads away from a liberatory, multi-ethnic vision of freedom. How do we gain ground in the post-Seattle, post-9/11 age, when the political climate is slanted against us?

These essays help highlight the continuing problems faced by both the revolutionary and still-embryonic anti-fascist movements. Despite important leaps, overlappings and mergings between these two currents, they often continue to exist in separate worlds. It's important that we outline some of the problems we see with these two camps.

All too often, the militant anti-racist and antifa scenes lack a coherent or even pronounced revolutionary outlook. We could even say that a large portion of it fluctuates between revolutionary politics and social-democratic positions, ending up with a type of militant reformism. Antifa are willing to fight, without hesitation, and have built up an independent culture that emphasizes self-activity: planning actions, building a base of support through music and publishing, being present whenever nazi or racist activity shoots up, and being permeated with a general anti-authoritarianism. These are all-important aspects that need to be cultivated. The majority of the antifa movement, however, especially in the U.S., lacks a coherent critique of capitalism and the state. Some anti-fascist organizing even consciously stops short of promoting revolutionary social change, thinking that capitalism and its ills are here to stay. These antifa argue that we need to focus on beating the nazis off the street instead, and maybe in the process we'll gain a little bit of breathing room under the weight of this racist, patriarchal and thoroughly repressive society. But ultimately this is a defeatist politic that can lead antifa to embrace aspects of the law and order regime, even looking towards the state as a potential ally in some instances. This has to be challenged and defeated. As antifa, we have come a long way through the politicization and momentum of the last few years and our politics are now more radical than ever. But it's still not sufficient.

On the other hand, there is a tendency in the revolutionary movement to ignore fascism and treat it as a shadow on the wall. Many revs believe real fascism died in 1945 and is now a non-issue. Some revs go further, believing that antifa actually assist the state by diverting energy away from anti-capitalist struggle and that by struggling against the state and capital we automatically fight fascism and its potential. This logic sees only two forces in society: the bosses and us. It fails to grasp the complexities of class struggle, racism and the levels of privilege and power that are present and are held onto by those who have them. It also fails to see the antagonism between the state and the will of a popular, yet reactionary, movement.

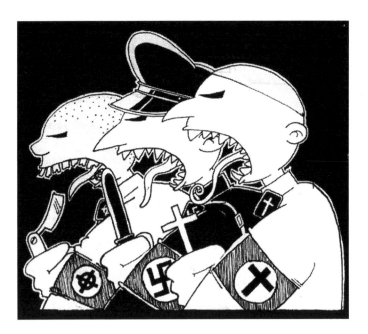

Another problem is that the revolutionary movement, by not incorporating anti-fascism into its program, may unwittingly embrace reactionary, racist
and even fascist aspects of popular struggles—and
not even know it. Or worse, they may try to deny it
while being fully aware of the slippery slope they are
playing on. Revolutionaries need to develop a more
complex analysis and, to be blunt, dump workerist
notions that there exists a united proletariat against
the bosses. The history of U.S. politics alone can
show the fallacy of this approach. White supremacy and white skin privilege long ago created differences in the working classes. Different strata of the
oppressed have unique and different class interests.
And 9/11 showed that there are forces outside of the
dominant boss class who have an agenda that isn't
pro-human or very proletarian.

A few observations (critiques you could say) that
we want to lay out now are specific to the essays but
should also be understood as a wider comment on
our movements. First, the authors are coming out of
a Marxist perspective, albeit an extremely unortho-
dox one. This makes for an insight into politics that is
sharper and refreshingly different than the majority
of the Marxist movement, and in general their perspective is uniquely different from most of the Left,
period. However, they tread lightly around addressing deficiencies in Marx's/Marxist philosophy, the
effects the last hundred and fifty years of organized
Marxism has had and the overall failure of the Left
to establish a free society. The potentials for emerging reactionary movements have to be analyzed
within the context of this history and the collapse of

the Soviet/Stalinist model of communism worldwide. Hamerquist and (to a greater extent) Sakai take a look into the defeat and/or degeneration of many movements, including those for national liberation. They also point out that what is left in the world today is far from the revolutionary socialist aspirations for freedom and equality that many of these movements claimed as their end goal (come on, everyone, can we say, B-a-l-k-a-n-s?). Marxism—and the whole of the Left, including anarchism—must be thoroughly reviewed and critiqued if we hope to create a movement of people capable of creating something new and liberatory.

Another major weakness in these works is that they insufficiently address the condition of women in relation to capitalism and fascism. Globally, women continue to be at the bottom of the pyramid of domination. They do, however, remain decisive factors in social and cultural development. Along with children, women continue to represent the largest block of exploited humanity, both existing as proletariat and still fulfilling traditional domestic roles. One is paid the lowest in wages and the other receives no labor pay at all, thus providing the free and accumulated labor that the whole of capitalist society depends on. The providing of this free labor, or the potential for an organized women's movement to take it—and the whole of their labor—away, could become a major factor in the future and itself could undermine the capitalist structure. But these issues are also at the center of fascist ideology. In an emerging fascist culture, the traditional forms of oppressing women become exaggerated beyond the point of recognition. The patriarchal nature of fascism places women in a particular class, or sub-class. Women become mere property, dominated and exploited by a male authority.

But herein lies the contradiction. The power of ideology affects all classes and strata of society. A fascist movement will draw its strength from both men and women. Hitler's rise to power wasn't merely the work of stormtroopers in the streets, it was made possible by the mass support of women. Hitler promised the creation of a cultural value system in which the contributions of "Aryan" women to the fascist German society would simply be child rearing and care of the home and hearth. A new proletarian slave class of gypsies, Jews and North Africans—made up of men, women and children—would handle the work previously done by "Aryan" women. All sexual

Women of the American Front.

elements outside of conceiving for the master race would be handled by state-promoted brothels.

Looking back at these lessons, what would the role of women be in a modern fascist movement? As is the nature of society, there will be contradictions and antagonisms to ideology and its implementation. Women will play a subservient role in fascist, patriarchal politics, but they can also act as active agents in its realization. Currently, the more sophisticated fascist and neo-nazi groups in the U.S. have and promote women as organizers, on par with their male counterparts. Aided by magazines, websites and how-to courses, a subculture of fascist women supports each other and promotes female participation in fascist activism. Will women play more extensive parts within reactionary movements? What are the potential developments here? How do we organize to deal with these complexities? What are the questions to be asked and priorities needed to combat both patriarchy and fascism? The struggle between oppression and liberation for women has to be placed at the fore of our politics and action.

In closing, we need to re-assert Hamerquist's theme: that the development of an anti-fascist politic is essential to the development of a genuine liberation movement. Clearly understanding the characteristics of anti-human politics and ideologies in all their forms must be prioritized. So also must be the struggle against them. Taking the fight to fascism—whether in its white supremacist form, in a crypto-fascist fundamentalist variety or perhaps even in forms we have yet to see—cannot be sidelined for the larger struggles, or vice versa. During the Spanish Civil, the anarchist militants fighting on the front against Franco's troops used the slogan, "The Revolution and War are Inseparable!" We take this to heart.

In this new era, the future is clouded with the still-shifting smoke and haze of 9/11. Our recovery process is slow going and filled with questions that seem to have no immediate answers. However, chances and steps forward can be had. What is needed is the political clarity to seize those opportunities and take those chances. We hope that these essays will assist in that respect.

For A Free Humanity!
Against Fascism,
Against Capitalism and the State!

FASCISM & ANTI-FASCISM

Don Hamerquist

This paper is directed towards a narrow audience of revolutionary activists who, hopefully, will not demand a finished product. It is not finished and probably will never be. Much of what I say will be controversial and is certainly open to challenge. On some points I would not be so unhappy to be proven wrong. I realize that I make a number of generalizations without what would normally be regarded as sufficient evidence, and I haven't adequately checked some of the evidence that I do offer. Feel free to shoot down any part of the argument, but remember that on the major points, validity isn't ultimately a scholastic matter, but an issue that will be determined and "decided" in struggle. Much depends on what we, and also the fascists, do and don't do.

For much of the U.S. left, fascism is little more than an epithet—simply another way to say "bad" or "very bad" applied loosely to quite different social movements as well as to various aspects and elements of capitalist reaction. But for those with more of a "theoretical bent" fascism in essence is, and always has been, a "gorilla" form of capitalism. That is, fascism is a system of capitalist rule that would be more reactionary, more repressive, more imperialist, and more racist and genocidal than current "normality" of ruling class policy. Many of those who see fascism as essentially capitalist also minimize the extent to which it is a sharp break with "normal" forms of capitalist rule. They see it as just the extreme end of the continuum of systematized repression that characterizes late capitalism. Often this is expressed in the view that capitalism contains an inherent drive towards fascism. A trip that some believe has already been completed.

In opposition to this position, I think that fascism has the potential to become a mass movement with a substantial and genuine element of revolutionary anti-capitalism. Nothing but mistakes will result from treating it as "bad" capitalism—as, in the language of the Comintern, "the policy of the most reactionary sections of big capital."

Fascism in my opinion, is not a paper tiger or a symbolic target but a real and immediate danger both in this country and around the world. However, the nature of this danger is not self-evident. It requires clear explanation and it requires the rejection of some conventional wisdom. Fascism is not a danger because it is ruling class policy or is about to be adopted as policy. Not even because it could have major influences on this policy. Nor is it a danger because of the "rahowa," racial holy war, that is advocated by some fascist factions. The policies of official capitalism carried out through the schools and the criminal justice and welfare systems are both a far greater and a more immediate threat to the health and welfare of people of color than fascist instigated racial attacks and their promotion of racialist genocide. The real danger presented by the emerging fascist movements and organizations is that they might gain a mass following among potentially insurgent workers and declassed strata through an historic default of the left. This default is more than a possibility, it is a probability, and if it happens it will cause massive damage to the potential for a liberatory anti-capitalist insurgency.

In this country, particularly, radical anti-fascists must be prepared to compete ideologically and every other way with fascists who present themselves as revolutionary and anti-capitalist and who orient towards the same issues and constituencies as the left. This is not to deny that capitalist reaction exists within and influences fascist movements, perhaps even decisively in some places and at some times (Eastern Europe?). However, I think that both logic and evidence supports the conclusion that this side of fascism is on the wane in this country and in many other areas of the so-called developed world.

HISTORY

When fascist movements, theories, and governments emerged following WWI, the common left view was that, in essence, they were a policy of capitalist reaction intended to counter the possibility of a serious working class challenge to capital. Of course, fascism was seen as more than a normal capitalist policy option—like tight money or protectionism. It was a "policy," but one that had relatively autonomous popular support. It was a policy, but one advanced by the most reactionary neanderthal wing of capital, while the "liberal" "progressive" wing opposed it, putting fascism at the center of major disputes within the ruling class. This position cut across the ideological spectrum, and was even expressed by major anarchist leaders; e.g., Durruti, "When the bourgeoisie sees power slipping from its grasp, it has recourse to fascism to maintain itself."

Features of fascism that don't fit this picture are normally ignored or dismissed as some kind of black propaganda from the ruling class. But historically these have been pretty significant features. Mussolini and Italian fascism developed out of the Italian Socialist Party and subsequently picked up some important figures from the Italian Communist party. German Nazis were national socialists and a large section of their following and some of their leadership were serious about socialism and anti-capitalism. (This is the Strasser-Brownshirt tendency that is the historical antecedent of the so-called third position, a growing factor in the current fascist movements.) Even the Hitler wing of the NSDAP was clearly anti-bourgeois.

From the early twenties it could not be denied that fascism had a mass base. However, most left analyses placed this base in competitively insecure sectors of the capitalist class; in pre-capitalist classes resisting proletarianization; and in essentially declassed elements, the lumpen, not in the working class. Any fascist influences within the working class were attributed to some extreme form of "false consciousness," or were discounted as the effects of temporary and accidental features of capitalist development (like losing a major war) which would be eliminated by the engine of history. At the heart of fascism in this view were, on the one hand and playing the strategically decisive role, the most reactionary elements of capital, and on the other hand a street force composed of gangs of opportunistic and essentially cowardly thugs. Fascism was a club over the working class, not a tendency within it. With the notable exception of Reich's position on the mass psychology of fascism, there was little serious examination of the actual and potential mass popular appeal of fascism.

This simplistic view of fascism was, and still is, paired with a simplistic anti-fascism. The main strand of anti-fascism was essentially social democratic. This stressed the need for a defensive popular unity against fascism premised on the general understanding that it was the policy of capitalist weakness — a final resort position for most of the ruling class. Since a complacent and comfortable capitalism would have no need to resort to fascism, the social democratic response (and the same essential positions were held by many who weren't organized social democrats) was to strengthen and stabilize "democratic" capitalism through the incorporation and institutionalization of trade unionism and the subordination of all struggle to parliamentary and legal considerations. The resulting de facto endorsement of liberal capitalism

follows right along the track of social democracy's increasingly reformist and evolutionary general politics. Not surprisingly, since they shared the view that fascism was essentially a form of capitalist rule that became more attractive to the ruling class when capitalism was in a weakened position, the Communists (Third International) ultimately wound up at a place quite similar to social democracy. However, before the eventual convergence there were important differences that demarcate a second strand of anti-fascist politics, a strand which at times has been very antagonistic to the reformist position even though it shares important underlying assumptions with it.

During the so-called "third period" of the late twenties and early thirties, communist orthodoxy posed working class revolution as the answer to fascism as well as to various other inconveniences, all of which would be eliminated as the byproduct of the elimination of capitalism. (The Italian communists who had early experience with fascism in power had significantly different positions, but in conditions of emerging Stalinism, they kept pretty quiet.) If this "left" anti-capitalist stance led to a temporary strengthening of fascism, that was acceptable — an attitude made famous by the German C.P. slogan, "After Hitler, Us." A parallel communist position of the period presented social democracy and fascism as two not so different sides of the same capitalist coin. Social democrats were "social fascists," and any strategic alliance with social democracy against fascism was excluded. In fact, there were examples of tactical alliances between Communists and Nazis against the social democrats. This is notwithstanding the well-known clashes between armed fascists and communists during this period. Clashes that are frequently exaggerated for reasons of post facto communist public relations.

Some of the positions taken in the debates about Spanish politics during the thirties follow a pattern similar to "third period" positions. Ironically these are often anarchist criticisms of the popular front governments, and particularly of the participation in these governments by the anarcho-syndicalist leadership of the CNT-FAI.

This "left" position is the second, much weaker, strand of anti-fascism. Elements of it re-emerge regularly as revolutionary groups see mainstream leftists evading confrontation with capitalist state power or even colluding with it, while undermining radical victories and potentials. All done in the name of anti-fascist and anti-right wing politics. This makes the "left" position understandable, but doesn't make it correct. At the present time such a position will lead to a serious blurring of the distinctions between the politics of a revolutionary left and those of various militant anti-capitalist fascist tendencies.

(Some populist and anti-capitalist fascists are already promoting a position of "left-right convergence," arguing that such historical differences are largely irrelevant and should be superceded. [See the Spartacus Press or other National Revolutionary websites for numerous examples.] On the other hand, the state and some flacks on the liberal left, are attempting to buttress the legitimacy and hegemony of capitalism by presenting a picture of a supposed "terrorist" merger of the extremes of left and right.

I will deal with this "left-right" convergence issue, both as presented by some fascist tendencies and as an element in capitalist ideological hegemony, at a number of points in the course of this paper.)

Shortly after Hitler came to power, and with Nazi Germany posing an obvious military threat to the Soviet Union, the communists made the dramatic change in anti-fascist policy and theory that is associated with the name of Dimitrov and the slogan of the united/popular front. No longer would fascism be defeated through the defeat of capitalism. Now, the policy was to defeat fascism by saving capitalism from its own fascist potentials and propensities. This would be accomplished by developing the broadest possible popular alliance—even broader than that envisaged by orthodox social democrats—around the defense of bourgeois liberty and bourgeois parliamentarianism. This period of the united/popular front against fascism lasted through the military defeat of Germany and Italy except for the brief, but historically very significant, reversion to a corrupt and hypocritical variant of the third period positions during the Nazi-Soviet Pact of 1939–40.

After the defeat of fascism in power in WWII, the Communist policy morphed into the familiar pseudo-strategy of anti-monopoly coalitions and anti-monopoly governments; focusing against the "ultra right" and relying on alliances with "democratic" and "progressive" sectors of capital for "peace, democratic rights, and economic progress." Hidden in the dialectical wastebasket is the classic Marxist tenet of bourgeois democracy being the preferred form of capitalist rule. The net result was, and still is, institutionalized support for a never-ending succession of capitalist lesser evils. Frequently this involves de facto support for the policies and positions advanced by the sector of capital that actually controls the main levers of state power. One of the more familiar examples of this approach in action in this country, was the support of both social democracy and the CPUSA for "peace candidate," Lyndon Johnson, against Goldwater in 1964, an historical moment when a challenge to all capitalist policy options was clearly developing momentum.

Insofar as there is thinking here, the underlying thought is this: first, fascism, rather than being a unique and specific danger, the policy of capital's extremity forced on it by its weakness in the face of adversity, becomes the permanent project of a "bad," "reactionary," "warlike," "ultra right" sector of capital. Bourgeois democracy; parliamentarism, constitutionalism, legalization of trade unions, rather than being a double-edged collection of questionable "people's victories," become the best possible terrain for waging popular struggle against capital, a neutral ground that must be defended against the "ultra-rightists" and fascists who would obliterate it. It would be possible to spend a lot of time on the history of these positions, and on various examples of their implementation, but for purposes of my argument there are two central points. Fascism was capitalism, but of a "bad," gorilla variant. Anti-fascism was either confined to the terrain of reformism or collapsed into the general struggle against capital. In the rest of this paper I hope to demonstrate what's wrong with the first point, and to develop an alternative to the second.

CRISIS?

The way we estimate the shape and the prospects of the incipient fascist movement in this country has a lot to do with our estimates of the prospects for capitalism. If we project a period of relative stability and balanced development, capitalist hegemony, particularly in the metropolitan center, can be maintained through ostensibly neutral mechanisms which hide the realities of domination and subordination. This will keep fascist movements (and likely the left as well) on the margins of society. If, on the contrary, capitalism is entering a period of major social and economic dislocation, a period of crises, the growth of the left, and, as well, the growth of fascist movements will be both a manifestation of the crises and a reaction to them.

There are good reasons why fashionable leftism no longer revolves around conceptions of capitalist crisis. We can remember the theories of "general crisis" and its various "stages." The predictions of the "final crisis" and of the collapse of the capitalist world system. We also should know what actually collapsed. There's certainly nothing wrong with delivering some kicks to Soviet "Marxism"'s simplistic economic determinism, but it shouldn't extend to accepting capitalism's unlimited flexibility by default, preventing serious discussion of the system's limits. While I don't directly argue the issues of capitalist crisis in this paper, I realize that the points that I do make imply a definite position that can certainly be challenged. Be that as it may, I think that capitalism, although superficially reascendent, contains defining and ultimately terminal internal contradictions. Of course these don't preordain a dismal capitalist future, or even necessarily give us the capacity to make specific predictions about this future. They do make it proper, even prudent, to assume a capitalist system that is crisis prone and crisis ridden. Carefully read, serious Marxism does not claim that capitalism will inevitably collapse or that it will be inevitably succeeded by communism. It claims that: "Capital itself is the moving contradiction, [in] that it presses to reduce labour time to a minimum, while it posits labour time, on the other side, as sole measure and source of wealth. Hence it diminishes labour time in the necessary form so as to increase it in the super-fluous form; hence posits the superfluous in growing measure as a condition—question of life or death—for the necessary. On the one side, then, it calls to life all the powers of science and of nature, as of social combination and of social intercourse, in order to make the creation of wealth independent (relatively) of the labour time employed on it. On the other side, it wants to use labour time as the measuring rod for the giant social forces thereby created, and to con-fine them within the limits required to maintain the already created value as value. Forces of production and social relations—two different sides of the devel-opment of the social individual—appear to capital as mere means, and are merely means for it to produce on its limited foundation. In fact however, they are the material conditions to blow this foundation sky-high." (Marx, *Grundrisse*, p. 706)

This "crisis in the law of value" is the reality that underlies the distortions and absurdities currently characterizing global capitalism. It is the stuff of the ecological crises, and of the marginalization of labor as well. It ties opulence to famine; medical marvels to epidemics; tremendous productivity to meaningless drudgery. This crisis does raise specters, but not only that of communism. Marx was aware of a different possible future, one that also is a specter, the specter of "barbarism"—of the "common ruin of the contending classes." Capitalism's current contradictions provide the potentials for revolutionary fascist movements, the basic ingredient, I think, of "barbarism," just as certainly as they provide potentials for a revitalized revolutionary left. It is not ordained that it will be a revolution from the left rather than an attack from the right that will "blow this foundation sky-high." Indeed, if we listen to T. Kazynski, and other less exotic advocates of deindustrialization, capitalist collapse might result from processes that

reflect neither left nor right goals or visions. This is why some very diverse political tendencies subordinate all issues to the preparation for survival in a post-collapse era.

There is no doubt that in response to these developing crises some elements of resurgent fascism will ally with capitalist reaction. But in my opinion these are unlikely to be the decisive and defining elements in this country.

Let's look at this as two different, though closely related, questions. First, is there a potential that a strategically significant section of U.S. capital would opt for a fascist state? Second, even without such a ruling class support, might a pro-capitalist variant of fascism gain hegemony over the various elements of right wing reaction and shape it into a unified mass movement that could impose fascism on the capitalist ruling class as well as the rest of society.

I want to focus on the first point in this section. However, the second point cannot necessarily be ruled out, so in a later section I will deal with the potentials of a mass pro-capitalist fascist movement without important links to any major sectors of the ruling class.

Obviously, if an important section of capital opts for fascism, it will have a major impact on the politics and the potentials of fascist mass movements. Even as it enjoyed greater visibility and more material resources, the cohesion and coherence of the overall fascist movement would be weakened by the defection of more radical and militant fascist positions. Its path towards power would orient towards coups and putsches and away from popular insurgency. To

varying degrees, this is what happened in the processes of the victories of fascism in Germany, Italy
and Spain.

However, we face conditions that are different in
major ways from Germany of the twenties and from
most other historical situations where fascism gained
a mass following and challenged for state power.
Germany after WWI was a defeated and humiliated
nation with a politically and economically shackled
capitalist class. In Germany, accurately or not, the
left anti-capitalist revolutionary potential certainly
looked real and substantial — sufficiently substantial
to force a reactionary unity on a capitalist class that
was in no position to respond to the working class
insurgencies with substantial pre-emptive concessions. Similarly, in Italy in the early twenties, and
in Spain slightly later, a large and militant anarchist and socialist upsurge faced a weak and poorly
developed capitalist class that could reasonably conclude that it needed to rely on the fascist card. In
these conditions a significant sector of the ruling
class did develop an interest in imposing a fascism
"from above," developing a relationship with those
sectors of the autonomous fascist mass movement
that were not genuinely committed to the more radical aspects of the fascist program. Despite this, even
in Germany, the nazi political structure had a clear
and substantial autonomy from the capitalist class
and the strength to impose certain positions on that
class. German national socialism was never just a
tool of the entire ruling class, or even of a reactionary sector of it. When this has been recognized by
the left, it has usually been viewed as something of

a "bonapartist" situation, which, though important for historical moments, is always eventually over-weighed and overwhelmed by the realities of class interests. Indeed, it is believed that exactly this tri-umph of ruling class interests occurred in Germany when Hitler crushed the fascist left wing in 1934 and made a compact with German capitalism. A paral-lel argument applies to Mussolini's accommodation with the Vatican and Italian capitalism.

The German left communist, Alfred Sohn-Rethel, infiltrated the top circles of the German Association of Manufacturers and much later wrote a book with an on the spot description of the actual relationships between the nazi movement and party and various capitalist groupings. His book makes it clear that the nazis had substantial independence from the capital-ist class even after the pro-capitalist right wing coup in the German fascist movement. This independence, according to Sohn-Rethel, went beyond bonapartism. He thought that the German fascist state and society were developing features that foreshadowed a new "transcapitalist" exploitative social order.

The most important of these features was fascist labor policy where, in significant areas of the econ-omy the distinctively capitalist difference between labor and other factors of production was obliter-ated. Labor, not just labor power, was consumed in the process of production just like raw materials and fixed capital. The implications are barbaric and genocidal and genocide was what occurred. But this was not the genocidal aspect of continuing primi-tive accumulation that is a part of "normal" capital-ist development. That type of genocide is directed mainly against pre-capitalist populations and against the social formations that obstruct the creation of a modern working class and the development of a reservoir of surplus labor. The German policy was the genocidal obliteration of already developed sections of the European working classes and the deliberate disruption of the social reproduction of labor in those sectors — all in the interests of a racialist demand for "living space."

There is no significant parallel between our situation and the conditions in which German, Spanish, and Italian fascism developed. U.S. centered capital is triumphant on a global scale, not defeated and disorganized. Its main concern is to avoid unnecessary disruptions to its hegemony, and if it were to support the fascist option, particularly in this country, it would obviously be just such a disruption. We might hope differently, but no significant internal or external challenges from the left are pushing U.S.-centered capitalism towards such acts of desperation. Some more or less marginalized sections of the ruling class (e.g. Millikin?) might develop ties to fascist movements and provide resources that could help coalesce a reactionary right bloc. However, this would only happen at the cost of diluting and undermining the militance and radicalism of the fascist constituency, channeling it into reformist and parliamentary arenas where it will have difficulty moving beyond pressure group status. We can hope that the fascists will be as blind to the dangers of this course as much of the left certainly is, but, as I will show in the course of this paper, we had better not depend on it.

NATURE OF FASCIST DANGER

It is easy for U.S. anti-fascists to be lulled into complacency because of the historic stupidities and religiosity of fascist groupings in this country. But fascists who can think are emerging, and as they do, there will be a base for their kind of thinking. The emerging fascist movement for which we must prepare, will be rooted in populist nationalist anti-capitalism and will have an intransigent hostility to various state and supra-state institutions. The essence of anti-fascist organizing must be the development of a left bloc that can successfully compete with such fascists, presenting a revolutionary option that confronts both fascism and capitalism in the realm of ideas and on the street. As I have said, unless the left can become such an alternative, there is a real danger that fascist movements will be the main beneficiary of capital's developing contradictions. It would be convenient if, for lack of an alternative, large numbers of people would automatically rally behind the left's various tattered flags wherever they got basically pissed off. However, in a crisis there will be alternatives to the left—fascist ones, and the left may very well not look like much of an alternative to capitalism. Sadly it will not only be hard to distinguish the U.S. left from various liberal capitalist factions, the lines between it and some of the fascists are also likely to be pretty indistinct.

Nevertheless, most of the U.S. left operates on the unstated assumption that in any competition with fascists for popular support we win by default. When the secondary issues underlying this assumption are eliminated, two main grounds for it remain. The first is the belief that all of the significant fascists will eventually expose themselves as pro-capitalist. The second is the belief that fascism is inevitably white supremacist. I want to deal with the elements of this assumption separately and at some length. Of course, this separation is for purposes of discussion only. In reality white supremacy and support for capitalism are normally linked. In this country, white supremacy has been a central factor in capitalist social control, and it is certain that any white fascist movement in the U.S. that was not categorically opposed to capitalism would be white supremacist.

People are not stupid and unable to see political reality. To the contrary, they are smart and see the truth more clearly than the left. This extends beyond

the popular view that leftists are just another species of politician to a basic skepticism about the left's
vision of the revolutionary alternative to capitalism.
Don't forget that the left is saddled in the popular
consciousness with the Soviet and Chinese models
(for some a treasured burden). These models look a
great deal like fascism to the average person. They
look a lot like fascism to many fascists, old and new.
Wasn't it Mussolini who said that the Stalinist USSR
was "fascism without a market"?

There will be no widespread popular confidence
that those who identify with the currently non-existent "actually existing socialism" in any of its phases
and permutations are reliable anti-fascists or that
they should be entrusted with power under any circumstances. Nor should there be. The truth is that
many left groups function like fascists—organizing
themselves in cultist obedience to a maximum leader
and proposing models of a good society that emphasize typically fascist virtues like discipline, loyalty,
and sacrifice. Other left perspectives are just liberal
reformism served with some nostalgic rhetoric. It's
not at all uncommon to find both features in the same
left organization.

Do we think that all of this has escaped popular
notice and will have no consequences? How could
that possibly be the case? It would not be difficult
to pre-empt the terrain of discontent from this left
of ours. Certainly this is more likely to happen than
that all of the fascists will decide to help us out and
become pro-capitalist. Let's look at this issue in more
detail.

FASCIST ANTI-CAPITALISM

Following fairly logically from the position that fascism is just a capitalist policy option, the U.S. left (also the British or at least the old *Searchlight* people along with their many other blemishes) has tended to view the actual fascist and neo-fascist groups as more or less of a joke. Their political positions are treated as propaganda that should not to be taken seriously, as just a cover for an opportunistic mixture of thugs, nuts, and cops that is essentially in the pay of sectors of the capitalist ruling class. Accompanying this is the terminally foolish conception of fascist cadre as cowards and bullies who will run from anyone willing to fight. Such positions should have died quietly a quarter century ago with the appearance of the *Turner Diaries* in this country. This novel, based on Jack London's *Iron Heel*, was written by William Pierce, who until his recent death was head of the fascist National Alliance and previously a major figure in George Lincoln Rockwell's Nazi group. The *Turner Diaries* is not a cartoon-Klan concoction. It elaborates a radical critique of the existing capitalist social structure and goes to some lengths to differentiate revolutionary fascists from reactionary, but reformist, right-wingers. Beyond a political perspective, the *Turner Diaries* lays out a moral and ethical framework for U.S. fascism which, whatever else can be said about it, is not opportunistic or lumpen. The left in the U.S paid essentially no attention and, with few exceptions, drew no political conclusions. Much of it is probably still, after two decades, familiar with the *Turner Diaries* only through its mention in newspaper accounts as a major influence on Timothy McVeigh, the Order, the Posse Commitatus, the Phineas Priesthood, the World Church of the Creator, etc.

Although the *Turner Diaries* were clearly revolutionary, they make a narrow and moralistic attack on what they picture as the essential corruption of U.S. society. Pierce is not enthused about anti-capitalism. His criticisms of U.S. capitalism focus on excesses and abuses, criticizing the alleged dominance of the financial element over the productive (sic) element. William Pierce was totally aligned with the Hitler wing of the Nazi spectrum. His politics rested on a mix of anti-Semitism, white supremacy, myths of a heroic white past, and other assorted aryan garbage. His vision of an alternative society was hierarchical, authoritarian, and patriarchal. This worldview may

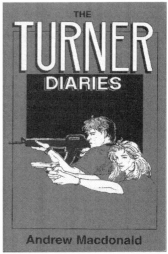

William Pierce led the National Alliance until his death in 2002; his novel The Turner Diaries influenced generations of far right activists.

find mass support in fundamentalist right-reactionary circles, but it has distinct limitations in popular
appeal elsewhere.

Pierce's attempt to create an American variant of
classical German Nazism has resulted in new fascist
formations that frontally attack him and his organization, the National Alliance, for being insufficiently
anti-capitalist, insufficiently militant, and far too
bureaucratic and hierarchical. A struggle is developing among fascists over whether they should try
to corral and capture the generic right or, alternatively, whether they should confront and challenge
right wing variants of reformism and parliamentarianism while looking elsewhere for a political base.
This provides a good place to raise a question mentioned earlier. Might an essentially pro-capitalist fascist tendency heading a mass reactionary movement
develop the autonomous strength to impose fascism
"from below" on a corrupt and weakened capitalist
ruling class? There is absolutely no doubt that this is
the intended and preferred strategy of the National
Alliance and a number of other fascist groups in this
country and elsewhere in the world. They would
like to gain hegemony over the massive amorphous
right-reactionary base and build incrementally from
this base towards power. (Of course, another part
of their perspective involves the penetration of key
institutions, the military and the police and the development of real military assets of their own.) These
fascists advocate both open and covert participation
in the Reform Party, in the Right to Life movement,
and in various conservative political and social movements in order to implement their perspective.

This strategy has obvious parallels to approaches of the traditional Marxist-Leninist left. Whether the strategy is advanced by authoritarians on the right or on the left, it generates the same sorts of criticisms and opposition. Capitalist development creates an anti-capitalist fascism that will neither retreat nor evaporate when confronted by what it sees as pro-capitalist fascism. Long before Pierce's strategy succeeds, it has created its own fascist challenge, a challenge that it will have great difficulty defeating or absorbing.

Which variant of fascism will prevail? Will they cancel each other out? I have my opinions but I could be wrong. What I do know is that, on this point as on all others, the most dangerous left assumption is that the easier road is the one that we will be traveling. The worst error the left could commit in this situation is to assume that Pierce's variant of fascism will ultimately prevail because it looks most like the best recognized historical model, German National Socialism. This assumption might ultimately prove to be true, but acting on it now only means that fascism will be effectively discounted as an ideological challenge, whatever significance it is assigned in other respects. This then becomes another support for an ultimately suicidal complacency about the left's own perspectives and visions. The only remaining question will be whether we get done in by the fascists or by the capitalists.

Some of the conflicts and contradictions in the fascist camp are apparent in the fascist music/cultural magazine, *Resistance*. Recently the magazine was taken over by the National Alliance, and its revitalization

and reorientation admittedly took a lot of Pierce's time. It is clearly an attempt to appeal to and organize radical white skinheads. In the first issues after the magazine came under National Alliance control some polemical articles by orthodox fascists led to an outraged and hostile response from the magazine's audience. One article criticized "undisciplined" and "tattooed" skinheads and argued that they should join the army and learn military skills. Another attacked the conception of "leaderless resistance" as infantile and amateurish. A further argument challenged any orientation to the "working class." The reaction to these traditional fascist positions led to the dismissal of one editor, and a formal editorial apology from his successor.

It is likely that Pierce's successors would have to modify his entire conception of white aryan culture if they want to seriously contend with more radical fascists for this base. I wouldn't presume to predict how this situation will ultimately work out. However, I do think that while the likes of Pierce might prevail organizationally and/or through force for a period of time, it is unlikely that they can win a conclusive ideological triumph.

THIRD POSITION

However unfortunate this was for him and his organization, Pierce's categorical critique of U.S. society in the *Turner Diaries* provided part of the impetus for the reemergence of the Strasser/Röhm "socialist" wing of fascism in the U.S., the so-called "third position"—a fascist variant that presents itself as "national revolutionary," with politics that are "beyond left and right."

(There appears to be two distinct wings to the third position. One calls itself the International Third Position, ITP, and tends to be more predictably racist, anti-feminist, anti-semitic, homophobic, etc. There is also a distinctly religious character to their politics. The other wing is called "National Revolutionary" or "National Bolshevik," and is much more radical; categorically attacking "Hitlerian fascism," and going to lengths to argue that they support all movements that are genuinely anti-capitalist. Some National Revolutionaries like the NRF in England are still overtly racist and white suprem-acist, despite their support for certain liberation movements; e.g., the Irish and Palestinian. Others, as indicated in some quotes I will introduce later, claim to completely reject white supremacy. Various National Revolutionary groups and ideologists also have differences about anti-Semitism

A FUTURE BEYOND LEFT AND RIGHT

that parallel their differences on racism and anti-imperialist national liberation. I would recommend that people look at the material of both groups. This can be done easily by beginning from the websites for "americanfront" and for the international third position.)

This third position variant of fascism poses a different and, I think, greater danger to the left than Pierce and the National Alliance. It makes a direct appeal to a working class audience with a warped, but militant, socialist racialist-nationalist program of decentralized direct action that has at least as much going for it as the warped reformist, nationalist, and pervasively non militant schemes of the established left. Not only does it intend to appeal to the working class and dispossessed — in distinct contrast to groups like the National Alliance; but at least some elements within it explicitly aim to recruit from the ranks of the militant left, and not from the radical right.

It is one thing to talk about abstract potentials for a militantly anti-capitalist brand of fascism. It's another to show evidence that something like this is actually developing. I believe that there is some evidence in this country and that there is a great deal of evidence in the rest of the world. The first indicators appeared when fascist groups began to move away from their traditional base in white racist reaction and look for recruits and influence in areas which the left naively believes are part of "its movement." I'm including a statement about the Seattle WTO demonstrations from our World Church of the Creator friend, Pontifex Maximus to illustrate this development:

"*What happened in Seattle is a precursor for the future—
when White people in droves protest the actions of
world Jewry not by 'writing to congressmen', 'voting', or
other nonsense like that, but by taking to the streets and
throwing a monkey wrench into the gears of the enemy's
machine. I witnessed some of what happened in Seattle
firsthand, for as chance would have it, I was in Seattle
from December 2 until December 5 to meet with Racial
Loyalists there and speak at the yearly Whidbey Island
vigil honoring Robert J. Mathews. I witnessed some
of the marches, and while there was certainly a fair
amount of non-white trash involved in them, the vast
majority were White people of good blood, who can be
mobilized in the future for something besides their economic livelihood or environment; their continued bio-
logical existence. It is from the likes of the White people
who protested the WTO (and who in some cases, went
to jail for illegal actions) that our World Church of the
Creator must look to for our converts—not the stale
'right wing' which has failed miserably to put even one
dent in the armor of the Jewish monster. Did the right
wing hinder the WTO? No. They were too busy 'writing their congressmen'—congressmen who were bought
off a long time ago, or waiting for their 'great white hope'
in shining armor who they can miraculously vote into
office. The reality, though, is that there is invariably a
kosher U or K on that armor. How many defeats must
they suffer before they realize that a change in tactics is
advisable? No, it was the left wing, by and large, which
stymied the WTO to the point where their meeting was
practically worthless, and we should concentrate on these
zealots, not the 'meet, eat, and retreat' crowd of the right
wing who are so worried about 'offending' the enemy*

that all too often, they are a nice Trojan Horse for the enemy's designs."

So Matt Hale believes, "It is from the likes of the White people who protested the WTO (and who in some cases, went to jail for illegal actions) that our World Church of the Creator must look to for our converts—not the stale 'right wing'." Is he just deluded? I don't think so. On the one hand, Matt Hale carries some baggage that would hinder his approach to our constituency, though the baggage is to some extent disposable. Weighing against this, he can appear to be, and probably is, more militant, more "revolutionary," and particularly in military

KKK and militia leader Louis Beam (above) elaborated the doctrine of "leaderless resistance" on the right.

Matt Hale (right) led the World Church of the Creator until 2005, when he was sentenced to a 40-year federal prison term for soliciting an undercover FBI informant to kill a federal judge.

ways, more effective, than the existing left. Hale's position shows the will and intent to break out of organizing approaches that have entrapped fascists before. We had better plan on the emergence of fascists that are substantially better able to exploit these initiatives than a hopeful, but frustrated, aspirant to the Illinois bar.

Consider the following passage from a statement by Louis Beam, the advocate of "leaderless resistance" and former head of the Texas Klu Klux Klan, who speaks to and for a militant, but more populist than socialist, variant of the third position: "While some in the so-called right-wing sit at home and talk about waiting for the Police State to 'come and get them,' some other really brave people have been out confronting the Police State, instead of hoarding guns that will never be fired, these people were out bravely facing the guns of the New World Order.

> "...My heart goes out to those brave souls in Seattle who turned out in the thousands from both Canada and the U.S. to go up against the thugs of Clinton and those who put him in office. I appreciate their bravery. I admire their courage. And I thank them for fighting my battle...

> "Soon, however, there will be millions in this country of every political persuasion confronting the police state on streets throughout America. When you are being kicked, gassed, beaten and shot at by the police enforcers of the NWO you will not be asking, nor giving a rat's tail, what the other freedom lovers' politics

'used to be'—for the new politics of America is liberty from the NWO Police State and nothing more." (L. Beam, *Radical Okie Homepage*)

The left had better begin to deal with the fact that issues that are regarded a part of our movement; "globalization," working class economic demands, "green" questions, resistance to police repression etc. are now being organized by explicit fascists and others who might as well be. Nor do we have a patent on decentralized direct action. That is exactly what the fascist debate around "leaderless resistance" is about. Finally, the question of who and what, exactly, is anti-capitalist remains very much unsettled. Some of the fascists take positions that at least appear to be much more categorically oppositional than those of most of the left. I said earlier that many third position fascists explicitly aim to recruit from the ranks of the left. This isn't as quixotic as it might appear. Indeed, elements of third position politics are hard to distinguish from common positions on the left, even from positions held in some of the groups that are closest to us. For example, some punks and skinheads who view themselves as working class revolutionaries, some elements of RASH, and even some participants in our own anti-fascist organizations are ambiguous on issues which should clearly differentiate right from left. These ambiguities, and actually this may be too mild a term, include romanticized views of violence, male supremacy, susceptibility to cults of omniscient leadership, and macho opposition to open debate and discussion with respect for individual and group autonomy.

There is a more serious similarity between third position ideology and the views of one important tendency in our section of the left. Various green anarchists advance a strategy of anti-capitalist de-industrialization and ruralism based on decentralized cooperatives. Various fascist national revolutionaries explicitly argue for a similar strategy. Of course, the fascists present this position in opposition to multi-culturalism and, more particularly, in opposition to immigration and foreigners. No significant element of the left in this country would currently accept these positions, although this may not be so true else-where in the world.

Even so, many U.S. leftists do believe that large sections of the population are so deformed by their patterns of consumption and by their acquiescence in relationships of domination and subordination that they cannot be considered as potential revolutionary subjects. This is a position which can also be found, not coincidentally, in such artifacts of the dominant culture as the movie, *The Matrix*. When the left com-bines these elitist perspectives with militant, but diffuse, actions against capitalist targets, the result can take on more than a passing resemblance to the "strategy of tension" admired by many European fas-cists and acted on by some.

Of course a major goal of our political practice should be to increase the "ungovernability" of capi-talist society. But this cannot be done without taking adequate account of the effects of our actions on the actual living conditions of masses of people. We have to recognize and criticize the elitism and arrogance in our camp that writes off large sections of people as terminally corrupted. Blood and soil fascists, who are mainly concerned with "their own kind," can, and do, treat masses of less favored people as redundant and mere objects. We can't.

FASCISM AND WHITE SUPREMACY

This leads me to the second source of unthinking complacency in the left view of fascism (perhaps Gramsci's term, "imbecilic optimism," is more appropriate). This relies on the assumption that fascism must be white supremacist. Thus even if it is granted that fascism might have some mass appeal, the argument is that this can't extend beyond the "white" population. The emerging non-white working class majority in the U.S., not to mention in the world as a whole, will provide the left with a solid and stable bloc, perhaps a majority even here, that, while it may be reformist, must be at least latently anti-fascist. There are obvious historical roots for this thinking, but it is dangerously wrong.

Two points: First, there is a real potential for working relationships and alliances between white fascist movements and various nationalist and religious tendencies among oppressed peoples. In no way does this potential involve the denial of the reality of white supremacy and racial and national oppression. It only means that the left cannot count on the responses to this pattern of oppression, privilege and domination fitting into its neat and comfortable categories.

Second, there is no reason to view fascism as necessarily white just because there are white supremacist fascists. To the contrary there is every reason to believe that fascist potentials exist throughout the global capitalist system. African, Asian, and Latin American fascist organizations can develop that are independent of, and to some extent competitive with Euro-American "white" fascism. Both points deserve elaboration.

Despite all of its rhetoric of "mud people" etc., even the WCOTC brand of white fascism could conceivably reach some level of tactical agreement with certain conservative forms of Black nationalism. This has happened before in this country and elsewhere in the world. Remember that even Malcolm X, met with the KKK while he was still working within the Nation of Islam. However, it is unlikely that such agreements would have more than some public relations significance. The same does not hold with respect to many of the "third position" fascists. They argue that their support of white separatism entails that they also recognize the right of other peoples to their own nations and cultures. Some of them deny that they are white supremacist at all and attack other fascist and racist groups for being white supremacists. Consider the following representative statement from the head of the neo-fascist American Front:

> "I am far from a White supremacist. To me a White supremacist is a reactionary of the worst kind. He focuses his energies on symptoms rather than the disease itself.

*The disease is the System—International Capitalism—
NOT those who are as exploited, often as badly or worse,
as White workers are by it. Yes, We actually see more in
common, ideologically, with groups like Nation of Islam,
the New Black Panther Party or Atzlan than with the
reactionaries like the Hollywood-style nazis or the Klan.
In the past we've worked with Nation Of Islam and single
issue Organizations like Earth First! and the Animal
Liberation Front when the opportunity arose. I'm sure
the future holds more common actions and Revolutionary
coordination between our 'Front' and others of like mind."*
(americanfront.com, Interview with Chairman)

Many leftists might dismiss this position and others
like it as contradictory and insincere, irrespective of
how many of them could be introduced. I wouldn't
deny the problems and contradictions that are

Neofascists assembling for terrorist hate rally.

inherent in the racial nationalism of the American Front. It is certainly possible that the "Chairman" could be spouting lies and disinformation. However, Black movements are already used to a great deal of contradiction and insincerity from the predominantly white left, not to mention mountains of hypocrisy. They are not likely to instantly dismiss expressions of political agreement and offers of solidarity from neo-fascists, particularly when they come with the prospects of material support. Nor will they be alienated by the explicit support of these fascists for the Palestinian struggle, the IRA, and the Zapatistas.

However, whatever the possibility for tactical alliances between white fascist formations and non-white organizations, this issue is not at the heart of the problem. As barbarism emerges throughout the global capitalist system one of its motivating forces will be the alternation of competition and cooperation among fascist blocs—with the competition dominating. In this country and around the world some of these fascist blocs will be, and, in fact, already are, Black and Brown.

Potentials that exist for a militant left exist for militant fascism as well. This is true in Uganda. It is true in Utah. If we limit our conception of fascism to Euro-American white supremacy, the only social base for fascist movements in most of the world, specifically in Africa and Asia, would be the atavistic remnants of white colonialism. We would be forced to another complacent conclusion, namely that only the left could develop a mass militant and anti-capitalist response in the areas of the world where the contradictions of capitalism and neo-colonialism are most severe. Such a conclusion would fly in the face of all empirical observation and of good sense.

Mass movements based in religious fundamentalism and various types of warlordism exist everywhere in the third world. They often have anti-capitalist features and frequently these have a quasi-fascist aspect. This should not be surprising. The crumbling structures of the national liberation states and the fragmented and demoralized elements of the communist movements in these areas are more likely to be fertile grounds for fascist development rather than a force against it. The foreign control of capital, labor, and commodity markets distorts the development of parliamentary and trade union traditions. The form of global capitalism that dominates in the periphery of the world capitalist system is not healthy terrain for the reformist leftism that predominates in capital's historic center.

The current situation of capitalism, its "crisis" if you please, impels a reemergence of genocidal tendencies in the capitalist center, a reemergence that is pushed by fascist ideology and organization around issues of labor and immigration policy and "eco-fascism." However, the really pressing danger of genocide is developing in Africa and Asia. On the surface it appears that fratricidal conflicts within neo-colonial structures combined with famine and disease are the cause of genocide in the third world. However, underneath these conflicts, hidden behind a careful hands-off public relations stance, lies international capital. The real responsibility lies in the essential acquiescence and the elements of complicity by the dominant sectors of international capital and the states in which its power is centered. If capitalism can survive the upheavals that these neo-colonial conflicts entail, no foregone conclusion, they will ultimately serve dirty capitalist interests by wiping out "surplus" labor. Whether or not this happens, this process leaves a substantial residue of fascist ideology and organization in the Third World, that is not restricted to the neo-colonial elites, but also exists on a mass level.

On a world scale, capital has largely succeeded in incorporating anti-imperialist nationalism through the neo-colonial bag of institutions and ideologies. In this country neo-colonialism involves important changes in class composition in the Black community. One of these is the development of a Black neo-colonial elite that is important to capitalist hegemony. This elite combines a sort of nationalism with little radical potential with pro-capitalist reformist ethnic interest group politics.

Any revitalized Black insurgency will have to challenge the Black neo-colonial elite and its ideology from a radical anti-capitalist and internationalist perspective. Beyond this, a revitalized Black insurgency will have to deal with reactionary religious fundamentalism and lumpen criminal organization. These are mass phenomena in Black communities across the country that already display fascist tendencies in their treatment of women and gays, in their attitude towards discipline and order, and in their use of violence and intimidation to limit and control discussion and debate. It must be said that a critique of the Black elite as corrupt and as betrayers of the interests of their people can be made by fascists. We are not talking about a critique from white fascists but from Black fascists with their own issues and agendas which, in all likelihood, will be at least partially hostile to those of white fascist movements and organizations. The revolutionary left in the Black Nation will have to compete with such fascists for the allegiance and support of some of the most disaffected and militant people of color. It does not portend well for this competition that maintaining "unity" and "morale" make some Black radicals reluctant to differentiate themselves, not only from Black reformists, but from Black crypto-fascists as well.

Historically the Black movement is at the center of every progressive development in this country. We certainly must hope that it has the resources to deal with these problems successfully, but we cannot blind ourselves to the difficulty of the tasks and assume that the right side will necessarily triumph in time.

MILITANCE, AND MILITARIZATION

While there is something left and radical-seeming about confronting organized fascists in a military or quasi-military fashion, this "hard" approach, besides being risky, often carries a load of conservative political baggage. Frequently this is the same old united/popular front—massing the greatest possible quantitative strength by developing alliances based on minimum agreements, agreements that are inevitably within the framework of capitalist hegemony.

There is no meaningful sense in which fascism can be strategically defeated while capitalism survives. Unfortunately for us, capitalism constantly grows fascists. Indeed, it is forming and reforming the social base for fascist movements at an accelerating pace. On the other hand, if capitalism were to collapse or be politically defeated anywhere in the world, this would not necessarily mean an end to the dangers of fascism. Under some conditions fascism might both contribute to this collapse and be its major beneficiary. So much for, "After Hitler, Us."

This is not to deny that fascism may present a real military danger, both in general and specifically for the revolutionary left. Effective anti-fascist organizing cannot be implemented without the development of a cadre with military experience and capacity. Anti-fascists must mount a military response to the actual fascist organizations if only for self defense, and there is no doubt that such activity may help organize our forces and raise our morale. This can be important, particularly in early stages of activity. Indeed, since military capabilities are essential assets for a revolutionary left, this is one reason to choose anti-fascism as an area of work. However, we must be aware of the dangers in this area and recognize that a military response will never be all, or even most, of what is needed to successfully deal with the fascist threat.

There is an important tendency in the anti-fascist movement to place the confrontation with, and the military defeat of fascism, as a precondition, perhaps an essential precondition, for an assault on capitalism. This looks like a variation on the Chinese strategy (at least it was once their strategy) of "protracted people's war." This is my reading of the RASH position, although it is all by implication and I would be surprised if in this case much is owed directly to Lin Piao, Mao and Giap. It is also the way that I understand the position of Britain's Red Action.

I think that seeing anti-fascist work as primarily military, and premising a strategy on the possibility of its military defeat is a fundamental mistake. The truth is that no genuinely committed movement can be permanently defeated purely by military strength even when that strength is overwhelming and has state power behind it. We know that this is true for the revolutionary left, we had better learn that it can be true for the revolutionary right.

At times the anti-fascist movement may win military victories, but these are often pyrrhic. While fascists may have been driven off the street in some situations, this is no ground for triumphalist claims if, as is often the case, fascist sentiment and organization keeps on growing in other forms. It is always possible that our "victories" are only part of a process of different fascist tendencies gaining ascendancy and working out new and possibly more effective tactics, ones that can minimize our impact. My argument here is not against militance and confrontation directed at the fascists and, for that matter, against the state. These are absolutely vital. It's against basing political work on shoddy and careless thinking, and forgetting that we should, "Claim no easy victories."

As Gramsci noted, in military tactics the emphasis is on attacking points of weakness and encircling points of strength, while in revolutionary political struggle it makes little sense to attack minor players and weak arguments. Politically defeating the weakest and wackiest of the fascists is not strategically significant. Neither are successful military ventures against isolated, unprepared or exposed fascists. Anti-fascist work in this country at this time is fundamentally a political contest with the fascists for a popular base. To do well in this contest we need to develop a coherent alternative to the fascist worldview that confronts the strongest points of its best advocates. Alexander Dugin, for example, not William Pierce or Matt Hale. Of course our alternative must simultaneously confront liberal reformist "capitalist" anti-fascism.

There is another exceedingly important consideration. The left and the fascists aren't the only players in these games. The capitalist state also plays a major role, but not one that is uniform, predictable and obvious. Notwithstanding the simplistic rhetoric of some leftists, the state seldom wants an organized and public fascist presence. Usually its public intervention is an attempt to ritualize and defang confrontations between fascists and anti-fascists, buttressing capitalist hegemony while making both sides look and feel a bit ridiculous. But this isn't all that is involved. Think back to Greensboro where a police informant apparently instigated the Klan attack on the Communist Workers Party, or to the Secret Army Organization fascists in Southern California where agents pushed plans for assassinations of left leaders. Along with cases like these where the state has promoted conflict by siding with the fascists, there also are situations where they let the fascists and anti-fascists "fight it out"—a preference that we have all heard expressed by various cops on the street.

However, it is still another possibility that I believe is the most relevant to us. The state can tolerate a certain level of anti-fascist illegality on our part just as well as it can look the other way at certain actions of the fascists. Currently, many of our "street" victories do seem to involve tacit police cooperation at a certain level; implicitly sanctioning, or at least not confronting, our tactics and

deliberately choosing not to investigate and prosecute at the level which would easily be possible. We
have to be smart about this. The behavior of the state
in this area is certainly not benign and it is not being
smart to think that it is unplanned and accidental.
However, when I read Red Action's self-congratula-
tory descriptions of its confrontations with English
fascists—and I have seen similar reports from various ARA sources—I don't see any recognition that
such success could only occur for a significant time
period with police acquiescence at the minimum.
Such "acquiescence" can be withdrawn at any point,
and, until it is, it can and will be used politically
against the anti-fascists both by the fascists and ultimately by the state. Keep in mind that in our confrontation with the fascists, the side that is identified
with the state is ultimately going to lose politically

although it may appear to be winning some street fights. And this is the least of the problem. We must also consider the possibility that the state is engaged in a more active counter-insurgency policy, a policy that attempts to determine the content of both the fascist and the anti-fascist movements and to keep the content of their interaction essentially encapsulated. (I want to come back to this point later.)

The left does have important advantages over all fascists, some of which will be mentioned later, but, generally speaking and certainly in this country, organized anti-fascists are at a major disadvantage in the military arena. Clearly the fascists have more military skills and a more substantial and better-prepared logistical network than we do. It is obvious that they are more able to draw on support and resources from within the armed forces and the

police. With time, if we have it, and effort we could conceivably catch up in some of these areas of logistics and training.

However, even if we did catch up, one fact still provides a military advantage for the fascists, even where they don't have such clear superiority in resources and training. Fascism is fundamentally a doctrine of justified force to advance selected special interests. Fascists do not worry too much about who and what is injured by their use of force. The left must, if it is to be true to a universal vision of liberation. When we abandon this vision and rationalize non-combatant casualties and collateral damage as the fascists might, the heart goes out of both our confrontation with fascism and our radical critique of capitalism. The prime beneficiaries of this will be the various liberal ideologists who are promoting the notion of the essential unity of the radical extremes.

This gets to the fundamental danger in overemphasizing the military side of anti-fascist work. A danger that is serious, whatever policy the state pursues. The "victories" in this area often have a major political cost. Combating serious fascist tendencies through physical and military confrontations is no joke. It requires a serious attitude towards internal security often including the limitation of discussion and debate and the compartmentalization of information according to "need to know" criteria. It requires a conscious decision to avoid those confrontations that might end in defeat or use up too much of our scant military resources. Since it could be fatal to rely on the state continuing to take a neutral or passive attitude towards such a project, security must be maintained against the police as well as against the actual fascists. Organizationally, there is an inevitable pressure here towards clandestinity. Strategically, the direction is towards military considerations taking priority over political ones. Under such circumstances the most dedicated organizers will often be forced to stand aside from potentials for mass militancy in order to maintain and protect a military potential. I realize that there may be situations when exactly this approach is needed. However, we should be very sure we are at such a point before taking steps that may be irreversible.

There are many examples of situations where the real or presumed need to function militarily has done much more serious damage to the movement than to its targets. This damage takes the form of militarizing the movement without conclusively defeating or, often, without even weakening the core politics of the enemy. Even within a best case scenario, militarization of the anti-fascist movement will always undermine essential political and cultural elements of our challenge to fascism, not to mention our alternative to capitalism. However, this best case example, one where we enjoy some military successes without major consequences from the state, is hardly the most probable case. In addition to the critical political damage that we do to ourselves by militarizing our movement, we could also suffer costly military defeats from the fascists, and major legal and political onslaughts from the system.

ORGANIZING SECTION

One argument of this paper is for a priority on anti-fascist work. It is important to put this argument in the context of an approach to political priorities in general. Sometimes mass popular movements dictate where and how we work and are ignored only at the price of sectarian irrelevance. But this is not the case at present, barring some major developments coming out of the Seattle WTO action. Instead there are a range of issues and organizing areas, all of which have legitimacy and potential and all of which present unique problems along with some common ones. Given the limitations in quantity and quality of the left in this country, not to mention those in our sector of it, there is no possibility to explore the potentials in every possible area of work. Since our choices between priorities will have to be made with no prior guarantees that they will turn out to be wise ones, we cannot forget the potentials and possibilities in the options that we have not chosen. If we do, our movement may rot in strategic dead ends, or, when we make necessary changes, they can appear to be arbitrary and even inexplicable, disrupt-

ing and disorienting the work. So what are the criteria for evaluating whether one area of political work or another should be a priority? I'll confess in advance to most forms of "leftism" and my position here will probably only be confirmation of this. I think that there are only two such criteria; first the extent to which the work develops a revolutionary cadre able to both think and act, and, second, the extent to which it helps develop a popular culture based on a core of intransigent anti-capitalism. I want to conclude this paper with some thoughts on the relationship of each of these criteria to anti-fascist work. I know that I am dealing largely with anarchists for whom vanguard party and professional revolutionary belong in the same out-basket as Moonies and cops. There are things to talk about here, but without dealing with most issues of party and organization, we can agree that it is important to discover and develop activists who are radical and militant and who are willing and able to formulate, implement, criticize and modify a collective political practice. This is what I mean by cadre. To the extent that the core group of cadre is growing in size and in capabilities, an area of work is relatively successful. If questions develop about changing the focus of work in an area, or even about moving resources to a different political priority, the extent to which cadre have been developed will determine how serious and productive the discussions are, and whether criticisms and disagreements can also be serious and productive and conducive to organized and collective changes in direction.

SPONTANEOUS ANTI-FASCISM

A substantial group of rebellious and anti-authoritarian young people is attracted to militant anti-fascism. The essence of this spontaneous anti-fascism certainly isn't an elaborated critique of fascist theories or a detailed understanding of the actual history of the fascist movement. It's more of a gut level rejection of the traditional fascist notions: who's superior and who's inferior; what constitutes a good life and what's corrupt. Fascists want a society and culture restricted to those they define as superior people. We don't. They want discipline and order; we want autonomy and creativity. Their goal is an idealized, basically mythical, past, we want a totally different future. They line up behind maximum leaders; we want a critical and conscious rank and file.

This spontaneous consciousness is a tremendous advantage for anti-fascism vis à vis fascism in all of

its variants including the most radical and anti-capitalist. The appeal of freedom and autonomy is far greater than the appeal of the fascist alternative of duty and self-sacrifice not to mention its cults of justified supremacy. Of course, spontaneous anti-fascism is more vulnerable when forced to deal with the emerging third position fascism that breaks with the traditional fascist verities and doesn't fit traditional leftist categories. However, even in this case the left has an advantage. The neo-fascists, even those who call themselves, "national anarchists," don't find it easy to separate from their history in a way that can give them credibility as a force for liberation and autonomy. Even more important, the racialist cultural autarky which is the root premise of even the most radical among them, looks more like unhealthy inbreeding than anything liberatory.

It is important to note that the national revolutionary fascists are aware of the historic weaknesses

in their position and blame traditional fascists such as the National Alliance who they bitterly attack for their failure to oppose all of the institutions of official capitalism. It's also important to realize that the left can easily lose its initial advantages, if it is so lacking in militance and anti-capitalist commitment that the problems the radical fascists have with their white myths, illusions about natural order, and various other aspects of ideological baggage can be overshadowed and overlooked.

The same radical popular consciousness is also a tremendous advantage for us against the hegemony of capital. Spontaneous anti-fascist consciousness does not see liberal capitalism and parliamentary democracy as the anti-fascist alternative. More typically it breaks with official society on many levels. Rebelliousness and anti-authoritarianism are directed at the schools, the police, the job and the family, not only at the fascist's version of the good society. In fact, hopefully, even if not quite accurately, official society is usually seen as a hypocritical masked paternalistic version of the fascist worldview.

This anti-fascist constituency provides an important source of revolutionary cadre. We have to go to it. It will not necessarily come to us. Of course, there are spontaneous potentials in areas of work other than anti-fascism, but for a couple of reasons they aren't as large and they aren't as promising. One reason involves issues of reformism and self-interest. At this stage of the movement, no one is genuinely anti-fascist solely from the sort of narrow self-interest motivations that plague other areas of radical organizing (including much organizing against the "right"). Fascism is rejected as a worldview and lifestyle, not because it is costing fifty cents an hour or something like that. As a consequence, many of the types of concessions and maneuvers that capital uses to co-opt and contain popular movements, approaches which are premised on appeals to narrow self and sectoral interests, have minimal impact on an anti-fascist movement.

Consider the main capitalist concession that can be offered to defuse militant anti-fascism—illegalization of fascist organizations, the terrain where liberals and conservatives debate the First Amendment. It is not hard to point out two facts to potential cadre, no matter how new and inexperienced they may be. First, the illegalization of fascist organizations can and will easily, and with pretty much parallel arguments, be turned against anti-fascist and revolutionary left organizations. Second, insofar as fascism is a real social movement, its illegalization is likely to consolidate its revolutionary credentials with its potential base and help differentiate it from, and strengthen it relative to, the reformist right—not something in the interests of revolutionary anti-fascists. Another potential of anti-fascist work is that, as contrasted specifically with anti-"ultra right" work, much of it is necessarily illegal or, at least, is on the extreme margins of capitalist legality. This dictates tactics and attitudes, and provides experiences that are important parts of the development of a revolutionary opposition. This work is good "practice" in a couple of different meanings of the term. In other areas organizing has a much greater likelihood of turning potential revolutionaries into reformists and/or cynics.

There is one major practical problem with anti-fascist work compared with other potential uses of the same human and material resources. The capitalist state and economic structures provide a permanent arena and relatively fixed targets for organizing. In contrast, in anti-fascist work, we appear to be dependent on the fascists having sufficient success to make them a real and palpable danger.

While capitalism, globally and nationally, will continually reinvigorate the base for fascism unless a left revolutionary alternative conclusively preempts it, at any given time or place the fascist movement may go through protracted periods of retrenchment or may embark on self-defeating projects. It is not a certainty that they always and everywhere will appear as a viable social movement, much less the sort of strategic threat that I have been indicating. There is little importance to symbolic anti-fascist organizing, or to muscle-flexing exercises against crackpots and dysfunctional teenagers, and at times it may appear that this is all there is to the fascist movement. This leads to questions about spending resources in what looks like a political sidechannel.

This possible dilemma strengthens one prior point. To the extent that anti-fascist work has developed a core of organizers, a cadre, the ability to make assessments and judgments that lead to a change in focus are improved. Whatever changes are called for can be implemented with greater resources and more clarity than would have otherwise been possible. However, in a more basic sense, it is likely that a weakening of the forms of fascism that we find relatively easy to locate and organize against, masks the growth of more sophisticated forms, better able to challenge us on "our issues" and with "our base."

One final point. Much left political work is essentially administrative routine and/or academic discussion. Out of this comes, not cadre, but more bureaucrats and professors, and we have enough of both. In the *Phenomenology*, Hegel puts the "risking of one's life" as a central part of the emergence of genuine freedom out of servitude and subordination. This is an important concept. A moment's thought will show that this element of risk and potential transformation is central to anti-fascist work, while it is pretty deeply buried in other arenas. Fascists are deeply committed to their views and are willing to kill and die for them. It takes some time, but eventually this imposes some serious thinking on anti-fascists, thinking which can lead to some of them committing to anti-capitalist revolution as a vocation.

CULTURE

This leads to the question of revolutionary culture, the other criterion for evaluating an area of work. I have argued that one tremendous advantage for anti-fascists is that the attraction of freedom and creative space is far greater than any fascist appeal to duty, self-sacrifice, order and certainly more attractive than racialist solidarity. Of course, this advantage is undermined by various authoritarian and sectarian tendencies in the left that are as hostile to freedom and creativity as the fascists, although they do not normally attack it openly. These tendencies pose obvious difficulties in relating to the spontaneous potentials of anti-fascist work.

However the limitations of the left are only the surface of the problem. Our main difficulty is not so much that we appear to be hypocritical, although we often do, as it is that our alternative appears to be utopian—to be a vision that can't work and that is fundamentally at odds with social reality. This view, that communism (or perhaps I should say, anarchism) is utopian because it is not based on natural order, on

1930s era Nazi poster denouncing decadent music; notice that the caricatured Black sax player is portrayed wearing a Star of David.

"blood and soil," is one essential ground for the racialist view of culture which is shared by all fascist tendencies, whatever their other differences. The same pessimism about the viability of the left's objectives is also at the root of the pervasive popular cynicism, and passivity. Needless to say, this mindset is actively propagated by the dominant capitalist culture.

Building a revolutionary culture means beginning the practical demonstration that our alternative vision can "work"; that it can survive as an organizing principle without being either co-opted by the dominant culture or compressed into a self-contained and essentially elitist "alternative." This culture must be something that is palpably ours, and that can remain "ours." This involves developing the internal resources to prevent insurgent cultural initiatives from eroding into matters of style and fashion and becoming merely a more or less skewed reflection of the dominant culture without the capacity to deal with the movement's internal problems and contradictions.

I don't feel able to do much more than indicate a few issues here. First, all fascists even the most radically anti-capitalist, view what they term as multiculturalism or internationalism as essentially degenerate and opposed to the proper order of things. The physical and social separation of people along racial and ethnic lines is crucial to the fascist worldview, even to tendencies that ostensibly reject the familiar larding of white supremacy. They all argue that society based on the opposite principles cannot work. Of course, passive acceptance of the inevitability of this same separation is normal capitalist common sense.

It is just as crucial for us that our cultural alternative

to fascism and capitalism challenge racialism. A revolutionary culture must be practically internationalist,
a space for the coming together of people of different racial and cultural backgrounds. Of course there
are problems and dangers in this and it won't happen without effort and conflict. It is one thing to say
that we have to respect autonomy and encourage the
expression of differences without abandoning the
attempt to build a coherent counter-hegemonic challenge to official society. But it is quite another to even
partially accomplish this in reality. Real conflicts and
contradictions are involved. They cannot be wished
or defined out of existence or resolved verbally. The
difficulty is increased because there are a number of
tendencies within our movement that are politically
opposed to it, for a range of quite different reasons.
Some believe, just like some of the radical fascists,
that freedom and autonomy are the fruit of the revolution rather than preconditions for it. Others basically question the attainability of genuine solidarity,
often for quite understandable reasons. Second, a
revolutionary culture must recognize the distinction
between and oppressed and oppressor and organize
against it practically. Much of the left recognizes
only one side of oppression, its impact on the group
subject to it—failing to see the centrality of opposing
popular acquiescence and participation in it. This is
a common position in the left and one that is shared
by the most radical and anti-capitalist of the fascists.
We can't allow a concrete opposition to the entire
range of oppression, national, sexual, and gender,
and specifically to the ways in which it is popularly
implemented and sanctioned, to be subsumed into

a generalized and abstract opposition to a common enemy, capitalism. Not only does this entail a certain approach to political work, it entails a definite obligation on the radical culture to practice internally what it professes as a social goal. Third, a revolutionary culture must not incorporate violence into its internal functioning. This is an extremely important distinction with all variants of fascism and unfortunately with many variants of leftism. It has to be a place where everyone feels safe, particularly those who are the objects of violence in society generally. This is not at all easy to combine with the importance of militance in the general struggle, with the necessity to reject strategic pacifism, and with the need to sharply challenge and vigorously debate various ideas and attitudes which inevitably will be a part of the scene.

WHAT WILL DO AS A CONCLUSION

It's been pointed out that in the form of an argument for a priority on anti-fascist work, I have actually been arguing for a certain critical stance towards the left that is not really dependent on accepting this priority. This is true, and particularly so in the final sections. Hopefully, if nothing else, the emergence of anti-capitalist fascism will be a "gift from Allah" (not my phrase but I love it), pushing the left to deal with the crucial weaknesses in its analyses and perspectives. If it isn't, something else will have to be found.

APPENDIX

This is a draft and, probably obviously, the concluding sections are particularly fragmentary. There is a group of questions that I initially incorporated into the body of the argument, but then it seemed to me that they made things too complicated and too confusing. However, I think they are important issues, so I've put them into an appendix on the relationship of fascism and capitalist state repression.

Obviously, my argument puts a lot of weight on the emergence of an anti-capitalist "third position" variant of fascism. It was hard to find a way to make this point while raising questions, which I think must be raised, of the extent to which that position is authentic and rooted, or alternatively, the extent to which it may be shaped by some repressive initiatives by the state. Even when we establish that the fascist movement is not in any important respect just an adjunct of capitalist repression, a lot of questions about the specific relationship of repression to fascism remain. Some of these require research and investigation. All of them require serious thought and debate.

It is undoubtedly true that state repression, including systematic population mapping and, more importantly, active counterinsurgency organizing under the rubric of anti-terrorism and low intensity conflict, is becoming more important in this country and around the world. While still attempting to maintain an ideology and rhetoric of harmony and equilibrium, important sectors of capital have come to accept that the potential for radical insurgency is a permanent feature of the political landscape, not an anomaly or an exceptional situation. Thus there are organized and sophisticated policies aimed at crushing, diverting or preempting such insurgencies in their early stages before they become serious challenges to capitalist power.

(Contrary to common left prejudice and public statement, none of the more significant fascist groups in this country make support for state repression the political focus of their work. This is in distinct contrast to the common positions in the reformist and legalist section of the conservative right. Parenthetically we might note that these are the elements, Buchanan, et al., that some reformists on the left see as potential coalition partners against "neo-liberal globalization." This convergence of reformism of the right and the left has more reality that any convergence of radical extremes.)

State (and supra-state) repression, particularly its new features, is increasingly important and must be understood and organized against, but it is not, in itself, fascist. Organizing against state repression as if it were essentially fascism will lead to serious errors. In this country for the foreseeable future, state repression will be organized to complement and supplement, and not to replace "normal" methods of capitalist rule. This is different from situations elsewhere in the world, where state connected death squads and para-police vigilantism are important features of fascism.

This is not to say that there are no direct and supportive connections between fascism and state repression. There is no doubt that fascist or quasi-fascist groups associated with LaRouche and the Moonies sell their services to both state and private capitalist repressive agencies. These services go beyond "research" and can include infiltration and disruption of left organizations. This entrepreneurial fascism is going to increase in importance in the capitalist center as elements of the ruling class and various capitalist enterprises maneuver to get around institutional legal obstacles to repression without obviously abandoning the so called rule of law. However, even this most dependent form of fascism doesn't conform to the common left view that fascists are essentially just a tool of one or another segment the ruling class, just mercenaries. They still retain their independent interests, both to make a profit and also, and more importantly, to advance their own political agendas.

A different sort of semi-relationship between state repression and fascism could easily develop out of some of the state's pre-emptive approaches to potential insurgencies. Privatized police forces or, more likely, the "pseudo-gangs" laid out in F. Kitson's theories of counterinsurgency, might drift out of the total control of the police and take on a semi-autonomous character overlapping with fascist groupings of more "authentic" origin. This has certainly happened elsewhere in the world; for example, in Colombia. The so-called "wars" on drugs and on street gangs provide a good basis for it to happen here.

However, the obvious antagonisms between emerging fascism and state repression are more important than any of these points. There is absolutely no doubt that some fascist groups are the objects of organized state repression in which they are treated not as criminals, but as potential armed insurgencies; just as revolutionary sections of the left have been and will be in the future. Even a rudimentary survey of the National Alliance, World Church of the Creator, International Third Position, and National Revolutionary literature makes it obvious that thinking fascists universally see both the state and the ruling elites as active enemies. The fascists pay a good deal of attention to the attempts to suppress and repress them and are attempting to develop a number of different approaches to counter them. Despite this, even individuals and groups that should be familiar with U.S. fascism persist in the position that the fascists are protected by the state and subsidized and controlled by the ruling class, and deny that they are the objects of organized and systematic repression. The way the state dealt with Bruder Schweigen (The Order) and the Posse Comitatus should have led the left to discard these particular prejudices, but apparently neither such facts nor the symptomatic glut of made for TV movies about heroic government agents penetrating armed fascist groups, can spark a light in that dim tunnel. I suppose it shouldn't really surprise anyone that a left that does not clearly understand or effectively deal with its own repression wouldn't see the repression of the fascist movement even if it was sufficiently motivated to look at the issue.

It's important that these questions be taken seriously and that they be addressed practically. The capitalist state and its repressive apparatus is a player in the conflict between anti-capitalist left and neofascist right. It has interests in disrupting and diverting both sides. It has interests is setting the terms and circumstances of their opposition to each other. I mentioned earlier that the state is attempting to buttress its own legitimacy and hegemony by presenting a picture of a terrorist merger of the extremes of left and right. Only the naïve would think that state intervention in this area doesn't involve active attempts to determine the politics of radicals of both left and right that go far beyond the development of liberal propaganda.

Let's look at a possible context for this state intervention. Shortly after the Nov. 30 demonstration in Seattle last year, some discussion began about the role of fascists in that action. In part this discussion challenged the common movement assumption that the left owns anti-globalization issues and stressed the strategic differences within the anti-globalization forces in the capitalist center, and between the center movements and those in the Third World. (E.g., "Aryan Politics and Fighting the WTO" by

J. Sakai, *My Enemy's Enemy* pamphlet by Anti-Fascist Forum, and interventions by Sleeping Dragon Press in Canada and by *de Fabel van de Illegaal* in the Netherlands.) Other contributions noted some significant and contradictory positions on the action from various fascist tendencies. Most of this discussion was helpful and potentially quite productive.

There was also a very different discussion initiated (to the best of my knowledge) by Morris Dees's Southern Poverty Law Center. They put out a so-called intelligence report on Seattle last winter entitled, *Neither Left, Nor Right*. The theme of the piece was that the Black Bloc in Seattle marked the probable beginning of a convergence between the most militant and (in the report's view) dangerous elements of the terrorist left and the violence prone fascist right. While the report presents no actual evidence of involvement of fascists with the Seattle Black Bloc, it does point out accurately that some fascists both in

Europe and in this country see the potential of organizing along these lines and that, in fact, with varying degrees of success, they have begun to do it.

The SPLC report clearly shares the common liberal criticisms of the Seattle Black Bloc's militance and anti-capitalist alternative to reformist protest politics. It also has the smell of cooperation between the "movement" and the state, something Morris Dees has been linked with many times, but seldom so dangerously. Predictably, the report has been adopted by traditional right wing "think tanks" that sell advice to various ruling class groupings and police agencies. For example, it is a major part of the factual basis for the Canadian Security Intelligence Service report entitled, *Anti-Globalization—A Spreading Phenomenon*. This purported left/right convergence will increasingly figure in official and semi-official propaganda aimed at undermining the legitimacy of the growing radical anti-capitalist tendency in the left. The issue, however, goes way beyond capitalist propaganda and disinformation.

This paper has tried to show that the notion of left/right convergence is neither a capitalist fabrication, nor a fascist pipe dream. Political tendencies from the less radical sectors of the left, as well as from the more radical sectors of the right, are attempting to organize around this line, sometimes without realizing it. Some revolutionary leftists are developing political positions that, irrespective of their intentions, appeal to radical fascists. I have mentioned this earlier in terms of *Green Anarchy*. There is real political momentum behind these processes and they must be fought intelligently and directly.

At the same time, things should not automatically be taken at face value. They can easily be something quite different from surface appearances. Keep in mind that we are evaluating positions that are often of indistinct origin and unknown strength, some of which may only exist in cyberspace. Some positions taken by third position fascists seem almost too calculated to enrage traditional fascists while eliminating one distinction after another between their variant of fascism and the politics of important segments of the left. These positions certainly must be disruptive and provocative within the fascist movement. They could easily play the same role within the left, if it is unable to develop an argument against fascist positions that are "better," certainly more radical and militant, than positions that are universally accepted as a part of the left.

Various elements of the repressive apparatus are certainly aware of the potential to manage and manipulate these developments to demoralize and disorganize both the right and the left. We should remember how such antagonisms have been promoted by state repression against the U.S. left in the past, and should carefully try to determine the extent that this may be an influence on both the fascist movement and on the discussion of "left/right convergence." Of course, this inquiry cannot become a substitute for actually confronting the political questions raised by third position fascism and by the limitations of left political strategy.

THE SHOCK OF RECOGNITION: LOOKING AT HAMERQUIST'S FASCISM & ANTI-FASCISM

J. Sakai

> "*The Superman is a symbol, the exponent of this anguishing and tragic period of crisis that is traversing European consciousness while searching for new sources of pleasure, beauty, ideal. He testifies to our weakness, but at the same time represents the hope of our redemption. He is dusk and dawn. He is above all a hymn to life, to life lived with all the energies in a continuous tension towards something higher.*"
>
> Benito Mussolini[1]

We weren't thinking about fascism while we watched two 757s full of people fly into the ex-World Trade Center. And maybe we still weren't thinking of fascism when we heard about the first-ever successful attack on the Pentagon. But fascism was thinking about us.

Fascism is rapidly becoming a large political problem for anti-authoritarians, but perhaps moving up so close to pass us that it's in our blind spot. Fascism is *too* familiar to us, in one sense. We've heard so much about the Nazis, the Holocaust and World War II, it seems like we must already know about fascism. And Nazi-era fascism is like all around us still, ever-present because Western capitalism has never given fascism up. As many have noticed, eurofascism even crushed has had a pervasive presence not only in politics, armies and intelligence agencies, but in the arts, pop culture, in fashion and films, on sexuality. For years thousands of youth in America and Europe have been fighting out the question of fascism in bars and the music scene, as a persistent fascist element in the skinhead subculture has been squashed and driven out by anti-racist youth — but come back and spread like an oil slick in the subterranean water-table. It feels so familiar to us now even though we haven't actually understood it.

While the scholarly debates about "classic" 1920s–30s eurofascism only increase—and journalists like Martin Lee in his best-selling book, *The Beast Reawakens,* have sounded the alarm about eurofascism's renewed popularity—existing radical theory on fascism is a dusty relic that's anything but radical. And it's euro-centric as hell. Some still say fascism is just extreme white racism. For years many have even argued that no one who wasn't white could even *be* a fascist. That it was a unique idea that only could lodge in the brains of one race! Others repeat the disastrous 1920s European belief that fascism was just "a tool of the ruling class," violent thugs in comic opera uniforms doing repression for their capitalist masters. Often, both views overlap, being held simultaneously. So we "know" fascism but really we don't know it yet. Once reclothed, not spouting old fascist European political philosophy (but the same program and the class politics in other cultural forms—such as cooked-up religious ideology), fascism walks right by us and we don't *recognize* it at first.

As fascism is becoming a *global* trend, it's surprising how little attention it has gotten in our revolutionary studies. Into this unusual vacuum steps Don Hamerquist's *Fascism & Anti-Fascism*. This is an original theoretical paper that has in its background not only study but fighting fascists & racists on the streets.

In this discussion of Hamerquist's paper we underline three main points about fascism:

- That it is arising not from simple poverty or economic depression, but from the spreading zone of today's protracted capitalist crisis beyond either reform or normal repression;

- That as fascism is moving from margin to populist mainstream, it still has a defined class character as an "extraordinary" revolutionary movement of men from the lower middle classes and the declassed;

- That the critical turning point now for fascism is not just in Europe. With the failure of State socialism and national liberation parties in the capitalist periphery, in the Third World, the far right including fascism is grasping at the leadership of mass anti-colonialism.

Fascism has shown that it can gather mass support. In many nations the far right, including fascism, has become a popular oppositional force to the new globalized imperialism. In many countries the far right

has *replaced the left as the main political opposition*. It
doesn't get more critical than this. This stands the old
leftist notion about fascism on its head. It isn't just
about some other country. Without a serious revolutionary analysis of fascism we can't understand,
locate or combat it right here. And if you don't think
that's a serious problem, you've got your back turned
to what's incoming.

FASCISM IN UNFAMILIAR DRAG

There is one thing we have to confront before we go
any further—the political nature of what is known
as religious fundamentalism. The stunning attacks
of 911 are being assigned to religious fanaticism, an
"islamic fundamentalism" that represents all that is
backward to the West. Ironically, both sides, both
the u.s. empire and the insurgent pan-islamic rightists, prefer to call their movement a religious one. To
the contrary, nothing about capitalism's "first World
War of the 21st century" can be understood that way.
Think it over. A supranational political underground
of educated men, organized into cells with sophisticated illegal documents and funding, who are multilingual and travel across the world to learn how to fly
passenger jet airliners and then use them as guided
missiles, is nothing but political. And modern. Pan-
islamic fascism pressing home their war on a global
battlefield.

The small but growing white fascist bands here in the u.s. picked up on this immediately. They had political brethren in the Muslim world. Politics is thicker than blood. "Anyone who's willing to drive a plane into a building to kill Jews is alright by me," said Billy Roper of the National Alliance, the largest white fascist group here. David Michael of the neo-fascist British National Party (which received several hundred thousand votes in the last local elections), was jubilant: "Today was a glorious day. May there be many others like it."[2] As one New Afrikan revolutionary always reminds people: *Like is drawn to like.*[3] Not race and not religion but class politics.

Why do we insist that some religious fundamentalist movements can only be understood as fascists? It isn't that the Taliban or Egyptian Jihad aren't religious groups. They clearly are, in the sense that their ideology and program are couched in an islamic framework. And they are part of broader islamic

Hezarat victims of Taliban ethnic cleansing in Afghanistan, August 2000.

rightist currents that contain people of differing political programs. Just as the German Nazi Party was part of broader nationalistic currents in Germany in the 1920s–30s that shared many of the same racialist views. People have tried to shallowly explain away the Nazis by saying that they were only extreme racists. They were that (which they shared with many other Germans) but they also had far-reaching fascist politics beyond that. In the same way, the hindu far right in India, for example—which contains perhaps the largest fascist movement in the world right now—is not only a religious movement in form but one which has far-reaching fascist politics in essence. There is no natural law saying that men's religions have to be benign or humane or non-political. And they seldom are.

But what the West calls "islamic fundamentalism" is not that at all. First off, like its brother "christian fundamentalism" there's some kind of relationship to religion but there's nothing *fundamental* about it. There's no similar vibe between white racist abortion clinic bombers today and some outcast Jewish carpenter with illegal anti-ruling class ideas in the Middle East 2000 years ago. And the Prophet Mohammad's youngest wife wasn't wearing a burka and hiding indoors, she was riding the desert alongside male warriors and disputing doctrine with male preachers as the head of her own religious school.

The modern islamic rightists, who began in 1927–28 with the founding of Egypt's Muslim Brotherhood, took religious ideological form but were started as a *political* movement against British neo-colonial domination. They were backed not by workers or peasants but by the middle-class bazaar merchants and traders. The core of the islamic rightists from the beginning were not theologians but young men who had middle-class educations as scientists and technicians (like today's Mohammad Atta who supposedly led the 911 attacks), and who used assassinations and trade boycotts. One trend within this broader islamist political movement developed fascist politics and a definite fascist class agenda. The fact that everything is explained in religious ideological terms doesn't change the fact that their program and class strategy fit fascism perfectly. Perhaps that's the real "fundamentalism" that they have.[4]

Throughout the Muslim world, from Saudi Arabia to Egypt to Turkey to Pakistan, Western imperialism has helped maintain militarized neo-colonial regimes that have looted and deadended society. They have destroyed local subsistence economies of self-production for use in favor of globalized export-import economies. The number of the declassed, those without any regular relationship to economic production and distribution, keeps growing. The lower-middle classes keep losing their small plots of land, their small market businesses, their toehold in the educated professions. These are men who are threatened with the loss of everything that defined them, including the ability of patriarchs to own households of women and children.

This is the class basis of today's pan-islamic fascism, which demands a complete reversal of fortune. Revolutions where today's Muslim elites shall be in the prisons or the gutter and the warriors of fascism shall be the new class ruling over the palaces, mosques and markets. They are more than national in scope just as all revolutionary movements have been. Because they are in a fluid war of undergrounds and exile, striking from abroad, of retreating from savage military repression in one nation to concentrate on breakthroughs in another nation. And to them, the world citadel of globalization in New York was not an innocent civilian target but a fortress of an amoral enemy.

The key thing about them isn't that they're following some old book. It's that they're fighting for State power just like everyone else in the capitalist sinkhole. They upfront want to rule, to not work but get affluent and powerful as special classes alongside the bourgeoisie, to hold everyone else underfoot by raw police power. Whether it's christianity or islam or whatever they claim to be following, these are definitely political movements.

Take another example: There are ultra-orthodox Jews who don't believe in participating in secular politics. There are ultra-orthodox Jews who believe in voting into power conservative pro-religion governments in bourgeois democracy. There are even ultra-orthodox Jews who support the Palestinian liberation struggle and reject the existence of the state of Israel on doctrinal grounds. But while the ultra-orthodox zionist settlers movement in Palestine claims that it's about nothing but pure jewish religion, like any other fascists they swagger around with guns, proclaim the right to do genocide to set up their self-identified master race, have an economy based on expansionist war, crime, and enslavement of other peoples. They are publicly proud of such "religious" milestones as their bloody massacre of unarmed people praying in a mosque and even their assassination of the Israeli prime minister. These are only fascists in drag, and we should see that there's more and more of them in capitalism today.

Adding to the confusion is the question of what "crisis" is. We're used to thinking of serious fascism as a product of traditional capitalist economic "Crisis," an economic depression like the 1920s and 1930s. That was true, but it's not the only situation for creating fascism. Because under capitalism the success of one class is the crisis for another class. There is social crisis of capitalist success (as in oil-affluent Saudi Arabia) as well as economic crisis of capitalist smashup.

All through the post-World War II period up to the end of the 20th century, as Western capitalism was in a long rising curve of protracted prosperity and explosive economic growth, fascism was starting to grow, too. Because that period of imperialist economic stability—ultimately leading to today's huge globalized economy of the transnational corporations—was also a time of large scale *transition*, of sudden historical shift that pushed some classes and cultures towards obsolescence as others rose up.

Not Depression but *change* propelled by the development of the world capitalist economy. In the industrial North of England, for example, the entire blue-collar culture of the British working class was transformed as factories, mines and shipyards steadily kept closing year after year. A new white-collar yuppie boom economy produced the Americanized England of Tony Blair just as marginal employment and three generation welfare families living in public housing came to characterize many in the former industrial working classes. Remember that despite well publicized fringe activity, fascism never sank roots in 1930s working class Britain. The British working class back then remained loyal to their colonial empire and their own social democratic Labour Party despite the misery of the Depression. But it's a different world now, of classes feeling abandoned by empire. Widespread "Paki-bashing," fascist marches and now a successful neo-fascist electoral protest party are only small signs of things to come. In a chain reaction, the British town of Tipton that was surprised to find four of its Muslim youth fighting in Afghanistan with Al-Qaeda had given 24% of its vote in the 2000 local elections to the neo-fascist British National Party.[5] And Britain is only playing catchup, lagging behind as all of Europe is being tugged, pulled by the political shift towards the right in all its forms. Despite historic prosperity.

It is vital to theoretically understand fascism because the general rightist tide from which fascism emerges is the strongest mass political current in the world today, and we need to delineate one from the other.

HAMERQUIST'S MAIN THESIS

The main thesis of *Fascism & Anti-Fascism* rejects the traditional left view that fascism is just "a tool of big business," racist thugs in macho costume carrying out repression to the max under the orders of their capitalist masters. Hamerquist sees no short term danger, in fact, of a fascist period over the u.s.a. Or even a significant "racial holy war" led by white fascists against Blacks, Latinos, Asians, Indians, Jews, Gays & Lesbians or others anytime in the near term future. Instead, he sees the danger of a new fascism that's more independent, more oppositional to capitalism. A *"potential… mass movement with a substantial and genuine element of revolutionary anti-capitalism… The real danger is that they might gain a mass following among potentially insurgent workers and declassed strata through a historic default of the Left."* He sees fascism not as a brutish prop for major industrial capitalism, but as a possible new form of barbarism. With mass support.

That is the main argument, but the paper is also dense with related insights and questions. Unlike the old left analysis of fascism, this analysis catches the vibe of Ruby Ridge and the *Turner Diaries*, of Ted K. and the Taliban. But it's still flipping a new page to think of fascism as a rebellious, oppositional force to u.s. capitalism. We should get used to it — quickly.

This critique cannot deal with all of the ideas in *Fascism & Anti Fascism*. What we can quickly do here is, of necessity, somewhat ragged. We define fascism in relation to other modes of capitalist rule. Major points in *Fascism & Anti-Fascism* are explored, such as the meaning of the "left" anti-capitalist fascism vs. "classical" 1930s fascism; fascism's mass appeal and how "revolutionary" it is; whether fascism is "a tool of the big bourgeoisie" or has its own agenda. Midway into this, we dive into a series of brief historical discussions of German Nazism, since it is the standard case for any analysis of fascism. Throughout, we are looking at Hamerquist's work, putting out analyses of our own, but most importantly trying to open up more questions. i apologize for whatever difficulties the reader encounters in this preliminary work.

VALUING NEW IDEAS

Fascism & Anti-Fascism brings several important understandings to us. It roots out the unpleasant fact that the movement is still using the old left's failed theories about fascism & anti-fascism from the 1920s. And that these old left ideas are really dead. This alone would make it worthwhile. In a movement that is long on stacks of little newspapers and short on new ideas, this is radical theory with an edge. Old failed ideas have their disguises pulled off, while we are helped to refocus on the realities of a postmodern future. What the author intends is to spark off a long overdue housecleaning of anti-fascism's dusty political attic.

Hamerquist's second contribution is to emphasize how fascism has its own life, and can be influenced by but is independent of the big bourgeoisie. Fascism is a populist right revolution that has arisen in the past from left sources as well as the far right, Hamerquist reminds us. He disagrees head on with the old left's position that fascism is just a repressive "policy" or strategy used by imperialism. In his view, fascism isn't born because some big bankers and industrialists give secret orders from a smoke-filled room. While the bourgeoisie can use or support fascism, the fascist movements are not ever neatly under their control. They're much more crazy-quilt radical, more grassroots oppositional than that. And once a fascist State is raised, this rogue tribe is even less under capitalist influence.

So this is a type of rightist challenge that has been an ultimate danger to us. Because fascism not only is an unrestrained violence against the oppressed & the left, but is a different class politics. One that infects and takes over masses of men that the left once considered safely either in its own camp or on the sidelines.

To me, one reason the left has preferred to think of fascism as only a puppet of the big capitalists is because in a strange way that's reassuring. Since the imperialists aren't really threatened by the tiny left here, they have no rational need to unleash maximum repression. Paradoxically, despite their front of condemning the government for being soft on fascists, the left in its peaceful slumber is actually counting on the imperialists and their State to be rational & keep fascism locked up in the warehouse. Counting on the capitalists to protect us from themselves, in other words. Hamerquist really picks up on this contradiction.

In subsequent sections, Hamerquist develops his argument that the left's

A theme that runs from the contemporary North American anti-fascist movement (top), back to German Communists in the 1930s (bottom).

smugness about fascism ("... *the unstated assumption that in any competition with fascists for popular support we win by default"*) is based on two misconceptions. The first is that fascism only comes in the traditional, opera costume-loving, Hitler-worshipping pro-imperialist type so quick to discredit itself. The second is that fascism can only be white and racist, so that any real fascist outgrowth here will automatically, like an alien cell in the bloodstream, be under mass attack by the New Afrikan, Native American, Latino and other communities of color.

Fascism & Anti-Fascism is valuable here because it opens up, in print, possibilities that have been discussed informally but not publicly dealt with by revolutionaries.

This is especially true when Hamerquist quietly points out that there exists the possibility that new white fascist groups might well find *"working relationships and alliances"* with *"various nationalist and religious tendencies among oppressed peoples."* And that *"there is no reason to view fascism as necessarily white just because there are white supremacist fascists. To the contrary there is every reason to believe that fascist potentials exist throughout the global capitalist system. African, Asian, and Latin American fascist organizations can develop that are independent of, and to some extent competitive with Euro-American 'white' fascism. Both points deserve elaboration."*

Fascism & Anti-Fascism isn't right on everything, but because it insists that our basic theoretical assumptions about the political situation are shaky & need to be questioned it is especially valuable to us right now.

MISUSING THE BUZZ OF FASCISM

The paper starts by stating that the left has no real analysis of fascism. Either it's just a label we attach to anything bad or it's only the repressive policy, the punishing puppet that the real villain, the capitalist ruling class, wields to hold onto power. Notice that in neither case does fascism exist as a real social development in its own right.

> "For much of the U.S. Left, fascism is little more than an epithet—simply another way to say 'bad' or 'very bad' loosely applied..."

This isn't merely an intellectual question. One of the important sub-themes in *Fascism & Anti-Fascism* is the realization that our present left theories and responses to fascism are actually the *same* theories and strategies that the European left used with such spectacular lack of success against fascism in the 1920s–30s.

This new generation of radical activism still has old basic ideas, and failed ones at that. Right now, everyone acts as though the word "fascism" is a free shot. So in our movement talk and propaganda we find racism, dictatorships, neo-colonialism, welfare cutbacks, repressive acts by bourgeois democracies, riot cops actually hurting middle class protesters at Globalization summits—all being wildly described as "fascist." One important reason that the German working class couldn't focus on Nazism is that the left had effectively watered-down the meaning of fascism, in effect convincing many to ignore the decisive fascist events as just more political musical chairs. Is the same thing happening here, right now? (It certainly has to folks as well intentioned as the anarchist black bloc, who were blindly led in the Anti-Globalization free for all into becoming the de facto allies of the white racist right.)[6]

DIFFERENT FORMS OF CAPITALIST RULE

This paper does have significant problems. As is very common in our discussions on fascism, *Fascism & Anti-Fascism* has no definition of fascism. So the obsolete old left views on fascism are replaced by good insights but also by a partial formlessness. Things are left hanging in mid-air, unmoored from the class structure and its basis in the means of production. Also, some of Hamerquist's most useful insights are overstated, perhaps underlining the discovery but also adding to the theoretical confusion. There is a relationship between these two problems, as we shall see.

Fascism is the newest of the forms of capitalist rule that we have encountered so far. We need to place fascism in context by first discussing it & other forms of capitalist rule, starting with a baseline of **bourgeois democracy.**

While modern capitalism strives to blur the distinction between two very different things—bourgeois democracy and democratic rights—at its heart bourgeois democracy simply means "democracy for the bourgeois." Remember, it was alive and robust long before there were any modern democratic rights at all. For several centuries in the English-speaking world, bourgeois democracy with elections, political parties and legislatures co-existed effortlessly with the chattel slavery of tens of millions, genocidal wars and colonial exploitation of indigenous peoples, the subordinate status of all women as an intimate species of patriarchal livestock, feudalistic dictatorial rule over the working class, and a government voted upon by a small minority of white male property-owners. That was the *pure* bourgeois democracy, the undiluted hundred eighty proof thing.

Back under feudalism, the State was simple. The ruling aristocracy *were* the State, and ruled directly and personally. But this is not practical under capitalism. Would IBM trust Microsoft to make the laws? Both the relatively large size of the capitalist class and its ever-shifting composition, as well as their culture of constant warfare to the death vertically & horizontally within the class, forced the bourgeoisie to create an indirect system of representative government. So bourgeois democracy became the preferred form of government for the capitalists.

Even with all its constant stumbles, feuds and scandals, it is the most effective form of capitalist rule for their entire class. There is nothing new here. The renowned 19th century u.s. statesman Senator Daniel Webster was the open paid representative of the banking industry then, just as another important u.s. politician in the 1960s was actually called by his colleagues and by the press "the senator from Boeing." Others represent the coal mining industry, the weapons lobby, New York banking and so on. Bourgeois democracy lets capitalists of every geographic region, industry and commercial interest influence State policy, although there is no pretense of equality amongst them. This is the most "normal" form of capitalist rule.

While it is overused as a left explanation, it is also true that bourgeois democracy is important to capitalism for its cooptive features (however, capitalism isn't adopting a form of self-government merely based on what's good propaganda). In an earlier paper on fascism, Hamerquist noted that *"...the mainstream of Marxist tradition which has consistently pointed out that bourgeois democracy is the ideal form of capitalist rule from the capitalists' point of view. Its virtue is that class exploitation and oppression are masked by supposedly objective and neutral institutions and processes: the market, the parliamentary-electoral system, the legal-judicial system... The capitalist ruling class will opt for fascism out of strategic weakness, not strength."*[7]

The other "normal" form for the capitalist State is **dictatorship**. Which is not really the opposite of bourgeois democracy but rather its sibling. There are frequent situations where bourgeois democracy cannot function. While the bourgeois democratic State uses police and military repression routinely, in a major crisis the mass unrest in society or the breakdown in social order can effectively deadlock or paralyze the legislative State. In the imperialist periphery, in the neo-colonial nations of Latin America, Asia, Afrika and the Middle East where extreme social crisis is just daily life, ineffective bourgeois democracies and bloodthirsty military regimes seem to regularly relieve each other in a revolving carousel. As though their rotation in mock battles was itself a new institution, one that is losing potency all the time.

Many people believe that fascism is just dictatorship and vice versa, that the two are the same thing. But while fascism is dictatorial, it is a different type of dictatorship. Capitalist dictatorship can take various forms, from military juntas to clerical capitalist police states to monarchy. But in general dictatorships use the repressive forces of the State to directly command society, sitting atop of the existing class structure. While fascism uses a violent mass popular movement to both remake the State and abruptly alter the class structure.

Colonialism referred originally to the system of colonies, which were commercial-military outposts of a nation in a foreign land. In Marx's day, "the colonies proper" meant populated settlements abroad still ruled by the mother country. As all major capitalist nations built their rampaging economies on conquest & occupation in the Third World, "colonialism" was used more generally to indicate the ownership of one people or society by another. Colonialism has been a feature of bourgeois democracy, obviously (in the pre-1960s u.s. South there was stable bourgeois democracy for settlers while the New Afrikan population lived under a reign of institutionalized terror). For that reason both the Black Liberation Movement and later radical feminism raised the question of "inner colonies."

Fascism is a relatively new and "extraordinary" form of capitalist rule. It first became a power as a new political movement in Italy in 1919. (Named after the *fasci,* the bundle of rods lashed together with an axe blade protruding from the top, used as the symbol of authority by Roman magistrates and standing for the imperial unity of the diverse classes of Roman citizens. The word "fascism" also had popular Italian connotations then of extraordinary emergency actions, of the Sicilian "fasci" of workers who revolted in 1892, of the democratic "fascio" that stopped the military coup at the turn of the century, etc.) **It is the twilight creature of a new zone in history, of protracted capitalist crisis beyond reform or ordinary repression.**

Fascism is a revolutionary movement of the right *against* both the bourgeoisie and the left, of middle class and declassed men, that arises in zones of protracted crisis. Fascism grows out of the masses of men from classes that are abandoned on the sidelines of history. By transforming men from these classes and criminal elements into a distorted type of radical force, fascism changes the balance of power. It intervenes to try and seize capitalist State power — not to save the old bourgeois order or even the generals, but to gut and violently reorganize society for itself as new parasitic State classes. *Capitalism is restabilized but the bourgeoisie pays the price of temporarily no longer ruling the capitalist State.* That is, there is a capitalist state but bourgeois rule is interrupted. As Hamerquist understands, the old left theory that fascism is only a "tool of the bourgeoisie" led to disasters because it way underestimated the radical power of fascism as a mass force. Fascism not only has a distinctive class base but it has a class agenda. That is, its revolution does not leave society or the class relations of production unchanged.

Fascism has definite characteristics that are both so familiar and exotic, because it combines elements from all past human history in a new form that is startlingly brutal and dis-visionary. **Indeed, fascism *never* appears in public as its secret parasitic self but always in some other grandiose guise.** Like the original fascism of Mussolini's Italy claimed to be the virile modernist recreation of the ancient Roman Empire. The Nazi Party claimed to be the recreation of the Nordic race of Aryan warriors (that never actually existed in human history, of course). The Taliban—who proudly brought order to the streets just as Mussolini's first fascist regime did—claim to be the recreation of the original islamic followers of the days of the Prophet Mohammed. None of these

Mussolini poses beside statue of Julius Caesar.

guises are in the least bit true, of course, but are closer to political fantasy played with real guns for real stakes.

This fascism has definite characteristics, whether in Nazi Germany or the Taliban's Afghanistan or the u.s. Aryan Brotherhood: It taps into and is filled with revolutionary anger against the bourgeoisie, but in distorted form. There is a supreme leader over a State that is not merely hierarchical but that tries to absorb *all* other organized activity of society into itself. The reason that Mussolini coined the word "totalitarian" to describe his vision of the State-society; and the reason that the Nazi State banned all sports groups, unions, professional associations, women's groups, lay religious societies, youth organizations, recreational groups, etc. except its own National Socialist forms. Same with the Taliban. It exults in the violent military experience that is said to be "natural" for men, while scorning the soft cowardly life of the bourgeois businessmen and intellectuals and politicians. (The Italian fascists put a key motto up on billboards and public buildings: "CREDERE OBBEDIRE COMBATTERE"—"Believe Obey Fight.")[8]

Along with that it raises repression to a new level by overturning the class structure, recruiting millions of men into new parasitic State warrior and administrator classes that are outside of production but live on top of it. It was early 18th century euro-capitalism itself that first redefined women not as free citizens and "not as patriarchal property of individual men, but as a natural resource of the nation-State." Fascism exalts this, and makes of women a semi-slave resource of the State restricted to the margins of an essentially male society.

One part of this discussion is whether political movements or social phenomenon can be said to have gender. Yes, fascism appeals to women as well as men. Yes, Nazism owed much to German women, no matter how unwilling feminists now are to admit that. But we have said "men" so often when discussing fascism because we are being literal. It is a male movement, both in its composition and most importantly in its inner worldview. This is beyond discrimination or sexism, really. Fascism is nakedly a world of men. This is one of the sources of its cultural appeal.

While usual classes are engaged in economic production and distribution, fascism to support its heightened parasitism is driven to develop a lumpen-capitalist economy more focused on criminality, war, looting and enslavement. In its highest development, as in Nazi Germany, fascism eliminates the dangerous class contradiction of the old working class by socially dispersing & wiping it out as a class, replacing its labor with a new unfree proletariat of women, colonial prisoners and slaves. The "extraordinary" culture of the developed fascist State is like a nightmare vision of extreme capitalism, but the big bourgeoisie themselves do not have it under control. That is its unique characteristic.

Fascism exists in a wide spectrum of development besides the well known State examples of fascist Italy and Germany. From politicalized criminal gangs and far right politicians operating tactically inside the constraints of bourgeois democracy to various nationalist movements and informal ethnic quasi-States. There are a number of examples of the latter just in the u.s., thanks to the u.s. government policy of using seriously fascist groups to control "minorities."

For example, last year an opportunist merchant in "Little Saigon" in the Los Angeles area tried to cash in on "normalization" of u.s.-Vietnamese relations by putting the communist flag in his video store window alongside the flag of the old Saigon regime. Mass violent protests ordered by fascist Vietnamese General Ky's subterranean regime/gang-in-exile not only forced the store's closing but ended the career of California's newly elected first Vietnamese state legislator (who had to quit politics because he had offended General Ky). General Ky's informal floating ethnic State may not have a geography or a recognized name, but it enforces laws of its own and regularly collects taxes in the form of mandatory "contributions" (to funds to allegedly fight communism). Incidentally, the video store owner first found his shop set on fire and then was himself arrested by the police for illegally pirating videos— do you wonder what the message was to the community?

And all fascist movements and leaders have their own particularities. The first fascist State of Mussolini was far more tentative and more conservative than Nazi Germany or the Taliban, for example, in part because the younger, less developed Italian fascism was weaker politically (and had to make major compromises with the monarchist army, the Roman Catholic Church, and the industrialists that Hitler for one didn't have to). The National Islamic Salvation Front that rules the Sudan both welcomed Osama bin Laden and his terrorist operation...and then couldn't resist robbing him of over $20 million (by their own admission). Poor Osama later complained to an Arab newspaper that his brother Sudanese fascists were a *mixture of religion and organized crime.*[9] So different fascist movements will not look exactly the same and might even conflict (just as the left does).

BEING BOTH REVOLUTIONARY
AND PRO-CAPITALIST

Fascism & Anti-Fascism has bold conclusions. i think that they are true in essence but not exactly in the way that Hamerquist suggests. A key passage in his paper is: *"The emerging fascist movement for which we must prepare will be rooted in popular nationalist anti-capitalism and will have an intransigent hostility to various state and supra-state institutions."*

This is really not a guess. Hamerquist is accurately recognizing the reality already on the ground, seeing without any old left ideological filters. This passage describes much of the current fascism that has emerged around the world. Not just small bands of third positionists in the West, but Osama bin Laden and the Israeli ultra-orthodox zionist settlers in the Middle East, the Taliban in Afghanistan, the "Anarchist party" in Russia, etc. New populist neo-fascists in the wealthy imperialist metropolis, such as Jörg Haider in Austria or the rapidly growing British National Party, are already anti-Globalization and anti-u.s. and could easily swerve much further leftward if the social crisis deepens.

But when Hamerquist says that this wave of fascism is both seriously anti-capitalist and revolutionary, i would have to qualify that. His insight is deep, but his exact breakdown is not and i think that serious misunderstandings could arise. Reading *Fascism & Anti-Fascism* too literally could get one disoriented, wondering if fascists are really "revolutionary" and "anti-capitalist" like socialists or anarchists are, then maybe anything can be anything and right could be left and oppressors could be oppressed?

The truth here is startling and it isn't in the least bit vague. **The new fascism is, in effect, "anti-imperialist" right now.** It is opposed to the big imperialist bourgeoisie (unlike Mussolini and Hitler earlier, who wanted even stronger, bigger Western imperialism), to the transnational corporations and banks, and their world-spanning "multicultural" bourgeois culture. Fascism really wants to bring down the World Bank, WTO and NATO, and even America the Superpower. As in destroy. That is, it is *anti-bourgeois* but not anti-capitalist. Because it is based on fundamentally pro-capitalist classes.

Fascism, in this slowly accelerating global crisis of transformation, believes in what we might call basic capitalism, *o.g. capitalism*. It is the would-be

champion of local male classes vs. the new transnational classes. Enemy of emigrant Third World labor and the modern supra-imperialist State alike, fascism draws on the old weakening national classes of the lower-middle strata, local capitalists and the layers of declassed men. To the increasing mass of rootless men fallen or ripped out of productive classes — whether it be the peasantry or the salariat — it offers not mere working class jobs but the vision of payback. Of a land for real men, where they and not the bourgeois will be the one's giving orders at gunpoint and living off of others.

Against the ocean-spanning bourgeois culture of sovereign trade authorities, Armani and the multilingual metropolis, it champions the populist soverignty of ethnic men. The supposed right of men to be the

Italian fascists from Forza Nuova (New Force) unfurl banner during Balkans war: "Kill Private Ryan"— the new fascism is "anti-imperialist."

masters of their own little native capitalism. In the post-modern chaos, this part of the fascist vision has class appeal beyond just simple race hatred alone.

Fascism is revolutionary far beyond that, and not as a pose. But by "revolutionary" the left has always meant overthrowing capitalism and building a socialist or communal or anarchist society. Fascism is not revolutionary in that sense, although it may use those words. **Fascism is revolutionary in a simpler use of the word. It intends to seize State power for itself.** Not simply to sit atop the old pile, but in order to violently reorder society in a new class rule. One cannot read *The Turner Diaries* seriously or understand Timothy McVeigh's politics (he was *slaughtering* the federal government not the Black Radical Caucus) without facing this. The old left propaganda that fascism is "a tool of the ruling class" is today just a quaint idea.

Cartoon from Louis Beam's Radical Okie website, 2002.

WORKING CLASS POVERTY
NOT THE ROOT OF FASCISM

This paper raises the danger of potential fascist inroads into the heart of its opposition—the working classes. *We would have to question this.* "Classic" German and Italian fascism demonstrated the ability to win over a mass base. Not just in general, but of a specific class nature: urban small traders and businessmen, craftsmen and foremen, junior military officers, significant parts of the peasantry (small farming landowners), petty government civil servants, the long-term unemployed or declassed out of the working class, the police and criminals. **To sum up, men of the pro-capitalist lower middle classes and the declassed.** Some workers left their class to join the fascists, just as some from the privileged upper classes left theirs to join the revolutions of the oppressed. But there is no evidence yet of significant working class support for fascism. While this question will be answered only in practice, by the struggle, it might be helpful to probe this now.

Fascism hasn't come from working class poverty or oppression. That's a deliberate capitalist intellectual confusion we have to get rid of. The oppression that colonial workers had to endure in Asia, Afrika, Latin America and the Mideast didn't produce fascism but hopeful, radical left movements of liberation that might have been ultimately subverted, but that also contained the constructive efforts of hundreds of millions of ordinary working people. Centuries of lynchings and police state terror and colonial poverty here in the Black Nation never produced anything like fascism, until neo-colonialism and what Malcolm X called "dollarism" took over. New Afrikan colonial oppression produced so many who were internationalist and forward looking, conscious anti-capitalists with integrity and democratic values. That really represented the historic Black Nation. A people that, however poor, however held low, were predominately working class and at the productive heart of the u.s. empire. A working class culture that had a lived belief in the importance of justice for everyone.

So don't be thinking that fascism just comes from poverty or recession, because it's not that way at all. In Euro-America—by far the weathiest nation that's ever existed since Babylon in biblical times—the growth of white fascism has nothing to do with poverty but everything to do with the crisis of white settlerism. So let's get two concepts overlaid together here. Even the imperialist metropolis is not uniform or homogenous. There are classes and economic sectors and geographic regions that are successful parts of the new globalized corporate economy—and there are those that are obsolete, cut off, part of something like an inner periphery.

For one thing, the u.s. empire is the largest of the historic European settler-colonial societies, but it is rapidly (in historical terms) being desettlerized by imperialism. That's why in the right-wing reign of President "W" (for "White") a Japanese-American general is head of the u.s. army, another Japanese-American is secretary of transportation, while African-Americans are secretary of state and "W"'s national security advisor (did you ever think you'd see a Black woman as the presidential national

security advisor?). NASA's chief of the technology applications division is a Black woman scientist and the head of ATF's anti-terrorism division is a white woman cop. In Silicon Valley there are four hundred computer corporations owned by Indian immigrant scientists. Oh, there's tons of white male privilege and white male preference here still and will be for generations, the continuing momentum of "the daily lives of millions." But the big guys are sending a message down to ordinary white men. *It's like a bomb.* In the new globalized multicultural capitalism, in the new computer society, the provincial, sheltered white settler life of America is going to be as over as the white settler life of the South African "Afrikaners" is. Forget about it.

Only, they can't forget it, many of them. It just sticks in their cerebellum. Settler America has never been really lower working class, remember. The mass of privileged white workers have always been in the labor aristocracy, a layer in the lower middle classes (the millions of immigrant blue-collar workers from

Eastern and Southern Europe in the early 20th century were not classed as "white" by Americans back then, but were said to be from inferior "swarthy" races).[10] And failed farmers like McVeigh's fellow conspirator Terry Nichols haven't been peasants (like in old Europe or Mexico) but a type of small businessmen. Timothy McVeigh can't be the real white man his father was, because the lifelong, high paying, industrial labor aristocracy of the steel mills and auto plants is shrinking not expanding. And he's not suited to be a softwear designer or patent attorney or tourist resort manager or any of the other good slots in the new yuppie economy.

Formerly, Tim would have been guaranteed security and respect as a white settler policeman or army officer, but he couldn't adjust to being lesser in the "multicultural" age of Colin Powells. McVeigh lost his army career despite being almost exactly the type of gung-ho noncom the military was looking for, because he couldn't stop fighting with his "nigger" fellow officers. Imperialism doesn't care if you are a bigot. Or if you make decisions on that basis just as the big guys do. Only you are expected to not be crudely upfront about it and cause them problems. Be a team player, as they always say. Only

WHITE MEN
Built this nation !! .

WHITE MEN
Are this nation !!!

White Aryan Resistance, 1980s.

the Tims can't swallow the humiliation of not being automatically on top as white settlers always have been before. To them fascism neatly takes over from settler-colonialism.

There can be many different kinds of capitalist crises, social crisis as well as a depression. The key here is the class loss of the role in society, in production and distribution. Men who are robbed of having a place and as a class can't go forward and can't go backward. Who are at an end.

Just as so many white farmers in the Northern Plains states know how to raise commercial crops, run complex farm machinery, juggle agricultural chemicals, negotiate government and bank loans in the hundreds of thousands of dollars for their own lands and business. But they really aren't needed anymore as a small business class (and the State is tired of subsidizing them). Globalized transnational capitalism can get cattle and wheat much cheaper in other countries. Most of those rural white men forced off the land and out of small towns, losing their independence as producers, make the jump to cities and ordinary jobs. Others can't adjust to losing their middle class feelings of independence (government subsidized, of course). However they manage to survive, in their hearts they are drifting to the far right as enemies of the State and the banks and corporations that destroyed them. Like at Ruby Ridge. Like the tax refusers. Like the very successful violent movement to reclaim federal lands for free local settler exploitation.

Even through the difficult poverty and insecurity of the Great Depression in the 1930s, the fascism that was raging in Europe found few followers here. *Because white settler-colonialism and fascism occupy the same ecological niche.* Having one, capitalist society didn't yet need the other. Nazism didn't do anything to Jews that Americanism didn't do first to indigenous peoples. And for the same reasons. **Settlerism has many points in common with fascism as popular oppressor cultures, of course. Which is the reason some Nazi theorists used white settler America as the idealized model for their Greater Germany.** When capitalism has abruptly de-settlerized before in other countries, a populist fascism has been one political result. For instance, when French capitalism

An OAS ("Secret Army Organization") poster warns that French President de Gaulle has a price on his head; France had abandoned its settlers in Algeria in 1961.

decided in 1961 to secure Algerian oil by abandoning the million French colonial-settlers there (at that time colonial Algeria was officially an integral province of France), a popular settler-army fascist movement immediately sprang into life that started bombings and tried to assassinate the French president and militarily topple the French State. That 1960s French fascism of the "colons" not only had mass support, but it still forms a base for the far right in France today.

Obviously, rightist political views that touch on fascism are held by many white Americans. They're conditionally loyal to the government (and *in* the government) only because their level of prosperity and privilege is so high that why should they lift their faces from the trough? But if the u.s. capitalist class left it to a "democratic" vote of its white citizens, known fascists like David Duke would be in the u.s. senate, there would be no WTO but also no Civil Rights Act, and much of America would proudly fly the Confederate flag of the slavemasters. The imperialist State's largest domestic security priority is not terrorism, the ghetto or the border as they pretend, but restraining and defusing white settler rebellion to the right.

So far we have not seen fascist movements based on oppressed workers (while workers are present in fascist movements, they have been outweighed by the declassed, lower middle class and labor aristocracy). Not only Al-Qaeda but the entire Muslim far right has always been centered in the middle classes and declassed, in country after country. Like all mass insurgencies, men from different classes may be drawn in but particular classes dominate the core, the cadres and leadership. In Syria, where a Muslim Brotherhood with a mass base actually conducted a violent terror campaign against the Ba'th Party and the Assad dictatorship in an attempt to seize state power, this class composition was very clear. The movement began in the 1930s with imams, students of the sharia, and small traders of the market. (In fact, just as in the Iranian Revolution these categories overlap, with many clerics earning a livelihood in the market as traders.) By the time of the Syrian civil war in the 1976–1981 period, an analysis of 1,384 political prisoners (most of whom were Brothers) showed that 27.7% were students, 7.9% schoolteachers, and 13.3% were professionals, such as lawyers, doctors, engineers.[11]

It is the classes dislocated out of productive life, the humiliated layers of middle class men who are angry and frightened, who feel they have nowhere to turn to restore their status…except towards fascism. Many unemployed college graduates in the corrupt and stultified Muslim neo-colonial world can always emigrate and become our $5.35 an hour clerks in the neighborhood convenience stores, or perhaps Western Europe's low-wage street sweepers and factory workers. (Like sons of former stalinist party officials in East Germany who are now prominently found in the nazi youth groups, they might have been on top but just lost history's lottery.) Some would rather say no and take the Trade with them. You don't have to like them to understand them.

THE "CLASSICAL" FASCISM WAS RADICAL ENOUGH

The discussion in *Fascism & Anti-Fascism* of the political differences within fascism today is mind-stretching and definitely educational. New fascist politics are being produced. However, the paper's elaborate scenario about the importance of the fight between the old "classical" fascism of the Hitlers and Mussolinis vs. today's seemingly more radical third position fascism seems questionable. Hamerquist writes: *"Obviously, my argument puts a lot of weight on the emergence of an anti-capitalist 'third position' variant of fascism."* To the contrary, i believe that his take on fascism today is essentially accurate whether third position fascism comes to predominate or not. He might be right about third position fascism—which stresses "socialist liberation" politics and makes a pretense of dropping racism—being the wave of the rightist future. But while a thin scattering of third position fascist commentators are attracting much attention, especially on the internet (and especially from their right-wing enemies in racist groups like the so-called Anti-Defamation League), so far they appear to have few soldiers. Every time we see any number of young eurofascists in public, they're the swastika-loving types we know so well.

Again, looking at fascism historically shows how it has always been very revolutionary, very radical, although not in the way that leftists are used to thinking of those terms. But radical and populist and anti-establishment enough to draw considerable support as an alternative to bourgeois rule. Which is what the question is here.

Here's the deal. The supposed importance of the defeat of the Strasser-Röhm "left" within the Nazi Party after 1933 was a big issue to many euro-leftists back then. It is the one slice of the old left position on fascism that Hamerquist still holds on to. But not only is it shaky factually, this view is clearly wrong conceptually. For one thing, the political meaning of that factional defeat has never been established — there is even some evidence that the Strasser-Röhm "left" would have been much *less* radical in power than Hitler and the S.S. proved to be. While intellectual Otto Strasser, who ran the Party's main press for years, and Captain Röhm of the "Brownshirts" pressed a more "socialist" line than Hitler, talk before taking power is often worth less than the paper it is printed on. Strasser's "Germanic socialism" seemed

Otto Strasser, once Hitler's "left" rival inside the Nazi Party. Shown in 1956 at the founding of his new German Social Union Party, which promised to continue the good side of the Nazi legacy.

to be mostly a collection of petty utopian plans and laws. After the war Strasser claimed that Hitler had only perverted the Nazi ideals, and set up a nationalistic social-democratic party in Bavaria.

Also, for all we know the only historic function of fascist "left" factions is to put on a more convincing public face to better lure embittered, anti-establishment men into the fascist movement.

But the most important reason that this line of thinking has proven to be wrong is because fascism in general — including the "classical" euro fascism — has proven to be violently radical & dangerously capable of attracting mass support far beyond the left's complacent expectations. Hitler is *still* being underestimated by the left. He was a brilliant, exciting leader who yearned for, fought for, dangerous changes far more radical than anything anyone imagined back then. *That his radicalism was of the right makes it no less radical.* Under his leadership the left was made to look pedestrian, dull, inadequate, as he crash created a shocking techno-culture of mass worship and violent mass re-identification. Hitler made millions of people change who they were. He left the bourgeoisie intact save for the Jews, but diminished its importance. He destroyed whole peoples, relabelled others and even eliminated the old working class. He reshaped Germany as a society for generations to come, and then destroyed an empire in titanic wars of his own choosing.

We forget that fascism has always been mainly a movement of the young. That many youth in 1930s Germany viewed the Nazis as liberatory. As opposed to the German social-democrats, for example, who

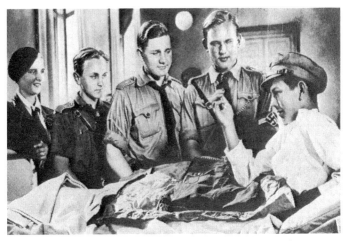

In one of Nazi Germany's biggest teen movies, Hitler Youth Quex, the hero rebels against his abusive communist parents to join the Hitler Youth, only to be murdered by a communist youth gang. Here he is seen waking up in a hospital bed surrounded by his Hitler Youth comrades, having survived his mother's recent attempted murder-suicide.

preached the dutiful authority of parents over children, the Hitler Youth gave rebellious children the power to keep their own hours, have an active sex and political life, smoke, drink and have groups of their own. Wilhelm Reich pointed out long ago that fascism in practice exposed every hypocrisy and internal cultural repression of the old left.

All during the rise of euro-fascism in the 1920s and 1930s, the left dissed & dismissed them as pawns of the capitalist class. Whether in the brilliant German Communist photomontage posters of the artist Heartfield or the pronouncement from Moscow that "fascism is the terroristic dictatorship of the big bourgeoisie," there was a constant message that Italian fascism and German Nazism were only puppets for the big capitalist class. This has some parts

Boneheads console themselves with a beer after defeat.

of the truth, but is fatally off-center and produces an actually disarming picture. Not that no leftists saw the problem, of course. In 1922 one German communist writer warned of a "Fascist Danger in South Germany," and even analyzed the Nazi Party as a highly militarized anti-semitic sect that was based in the petty bourgeoisie but was agitating against big business.[12] These assessments on the ground were soon swept away by dismissive theories from the big left uberheadquarters in Berlin and Moscow.

Today we think of fascism so much in terms of its repression, that we forget how much Nazism built its movement by campaigning against big capitalism. One famous National Socialist election poster shows a social democratic winged "angel" walking hand in hand with a stereotyped banker, with the big slogan: **"Marxism is the Guardian Angel of Capitalism."**[13] Hitler promised to preserve the "good" productive capitalism of ordinary hard-working Germans, while wiping out the "bad" parasitic big capitalism of the hidden finance capitalist Jewish bosses. In fact, tens of millions of Americans (and not just white folks) would support such a program right here & now. Fascism blended together a radical sentiment against the big bourgeoisie and their State, together with racist-nationalist ideology, into a political uprising of the middle classes and declassed.

The Nazi Party under Hitler was acting always under the pervasive hegemony of capitalist culture,

*"Marxism is the Guardian Angel of Capitalism
Vote National Socialist, List 1."*

but it was in no way under the orders of the former capitalist ruling class. It actually pushed the big capitalists away from State power, just as Hitler always promised that it would (Hamerquist strongly emphasizes this point).

The notion that big business interests push buttons to create or disappear fascism at will, as they need it, is an enduring left fable. It sounds so reasonable from a conspiratorial point of view, and generations of leftists have repeated it so often we just assume that it's true. But, you know, there's a special hell for movements that fall in love with their own propaganda. *We're going to dip into a discussion of fascist history to sort out these questions factually.*

It's true that Adolf Hitler didn't need a day job. He was the most dramatic new leader on the German political scene; one who had participated in violence

Sticker from the fascist group "Troisième Voie" (Third Way): "Neither the Dollar Right Nor the Caviar Left" (France, early 1990s).

himself and whose politics were not only outside of the mainstream but beyond the boundaries of the law. Once he got out of prison after the failed 1923 Munich putsch, Hitler was personally supported by the Duchess of Sachsen-Anhalt as he began rebuilding his party.[14] Party gossip then talked about "Hitler's women"—not mistresses but older, wealthy right-wing women who were charmed to have tea with the poetic, stormy young fuhrer in return for donations. And there were always some businessmen, like the Bechstein family of piano makers, who supported the Nazis. This level of support might square with, say, the support that the 1960s Black Power radicalism got from wealthy white progressives. The militant u.s. Black Power movement received large amounts of money from upper-class sources as diverse as the national Episcopal Church and one of the Rockefellers. Should we think that H. Rap Brown and Amiri Baraka were "puppets of the ruling class"? Or that their nationalist Black Revolution was a ruling class strategy? Fact is, many wealthy people have many different causes and hobby horses to ride.

The major German capitalists didn't support the excessively unstable, fractious, violent, anti-bourgeois Nazi Party until *after* its 1930 electoral breakout into being the dynamic major party of the Right. That is, after a long decade of difficult fighting and building from tiny, obscure beginnings.[15] The Nazis were a poor party by bourgeois standards, financed primarily from their own members and followers. Big capitalism in Germany had instead backed a rival party with big cash—the right wing but respectably bourgeois German Nationalist Party, headed by Alfred Hugenberg. (A director of the giant Krupp armaments firm, Hugenberg owned the major UFA film studios, the leading German advertising firm, and a nationwide chain of newspapers. He was supported by Hjalmar Schacht of the Reichsbank and Albert Voegler of United Steel.)[16] This is another way of saying that the major German capitalists themselves long misjudged how to handle the crisis that was destroying Depression-era Germany. This is no surprise, since their misruling class ineptitude was one reason things were in such crisis. The failures and misjudgement of the capitalist class leadership play a larger role in things than we sometimes recognize.

In particular, fascism has always developed a hard radical edge to it that called to the lower middle classes and the declassed to come battle not only the treacherous left but the bosses and their government (in the periphery this same fascist class politics is reshaped to an "anti-colonial" battle against Western imperialism and its corrupt local neo-colonial allied regimes). The "classical" Nazi fascism—which named itself the "German National Socialist Workers Party," after all—could get roughly a quarter of its votes in 1930 from the working class, although mostly from the long term unemployed strata.[17] But it was not based in the working class. Nazi Gauleiter Alfred Krebs of Munich reported that the party cadres came almost exclusively from the lowest of the middle classes (office workers, petty civil servants, self-employed craftsmen and traders), not from either the main middle classes or industrial workers.[18] Nevertheless, these new class fighters numbered in the hundreds of thousands and millions, a powerful political force. And anti-bourgeois politics were music to their ears, just as condemning the corrupt excess of Saudi princes and oil millionaires help attract pan-islamic fascism's followers. Nazi Gauleiter Krebs reported that *"any attack on capitalism and plutocracy found the strongest echo among the local functionaries* [of the Nazi Party — ed.] *with their middle-class origin."*[19]

Listen to Daniel Guerin's eyewitness account of a Nazi SA "stormtrooper" rally in Leipzig in 1933:

"Saturday evening at a popular dance hall in a working-class district of Leipzig. Men and women around tables, dressed like petit-bourgeois, like all German workers. There are many SAs and Hitler Youth, but here there is neither arrogance not starchiness; it's free and easy, noisy laughter — we're among the people. The orchestra, in uniform, plays good classical music: Wagner, Verdi. At the intermission, an orator mounts the stage and harangues the crowd, which is at first attentive and docile. The theme: 'Our Revolution'.

"'*Our Revolution*, Volksgenossen ["National Comrades"], *has only begun. We haven't yet attained any of our goals. There's talk of a national government, of a national awakening… What's all that about? It's the* Socialist *part of our program that matters.*'

"'The crowd emits a satisfied "Ah!" This is what everyone was thinking but didn't dare articulate.

Now their gaze passionately follows this man
who speaks for them all.

> "'The Reich of Wilhelm II was a Reich without an
> ideal. The bourgeoisie ruled with its disgusting mate-
> rialism and its contempt for the proletariat. The 1918
> Revolution, Volksgenossen, couldn't destroy the
> old system. The Socialist leaders abandoned the dic-
> tatorship of the proletariat for the golden calf. They
> betrayed the nation and they betrayed the people. As
> for communism, it's proven itself unable to get rid of
> them, since Stalin renounced Leninist Bolshevism for
> capitalist individualism.'

"I listen spellbound to this tirade. Am I really at
a Hitlerite meeting? But the demagogue knows
what he's doing, for the crowd is vibrating
around me at an ever-increasing rhythm.

> "'The bourgeoisie, Volksgenossen, continued to
> monopolize patriotism, to abandon the masses to
> Marxism, that dog's breakfast. For our part, we've
> understood that we had to go to the proletariat and
> enter into it, that to conquer Germany meant con-
> quering the working class. And when we revealed the
> idea of the Fatherland to these proletarians, there were
> tears of gratitude on many a Face …'

"This emphatic missionary language is followed
by diatribe and threats: 'We have now but one enemy
to vanquish: the bourgeoisie. To bad for it if it doesn't
want to give in, if it doesn't want to understand …'

"And carried away by his eloquence, he lets the
admission slip out: 'Besides, one day it will be grateful
that we treated it this way.'

"But the crowd didn't hear that. It believes only that the revolution has begun, that socialism is on the horizon. And when he has finished, it sings with raw anger:

"'O producers, you deeply suffer
The poverty of the times.
The army of the unemployed
Relentlessly grows.
But joyous and free worker,
Still you sing the old song:
We are the workers,
The Proletariat!

"'You labor every day
For a salary of famine.
But the Tietzs, the Wertheims, and the Cohns
Know neither poverty nor pain.
You exhaust and overwork yourself:
Who benefits from your labor?
It's the shareholders,
The Profitariat.'"[20]

Is today's third position fascism more radical than that? I doubt it. Fascism always taps into and channels the raw radical anger and class envy of lower classes against the bourgeois, in order to create a distorted revolutionary instrument. Not just as a trick, either. **This distorted class anger is necessary to sharpen the violent instrument that fascism needs.**

Nor was this true only in Germany. Fascism originally started in Italy among some socialist intellectuals, demobilized *arditi* (the Italian army's elite assault commando units), avant-garde artists & writers, and then young rural landowners. Their economic program was very "left" and against big business. Even as late as 1921, fascist leader Mussolini (the former pro armed struggle tendency leader of the Italian Socialist Party and editor of the party newspaper) was proposing that the monarchy and parliament be forcibly abolished, and replaced by a joint fascist-socialist-catholic reformist "right-left" rule over the nation. Although Mussolini explored this path towards power, it was too late already—as he spoke, fascist squads were killing leftists, burning whole villages that had gone "red," and breaking up unions. That is less significant for us than understanding his need to put forward the most "left" face possible on his way to State power. Mussolini even spoke favorably about the spontaneous workers councils movement that was taking over factories and calling for anti-capitalist revolution:

> "No social transformation which is necessary is repugnant to me. Hence I accept the famous workers' supervision of the factories and equally their cooperative social management; I only ask that there should be a clear conscience and technical capacity, and that production be increased. If this is guaranteed by the trade unions, instead of by the employers, I have no hesitation in saying that the former have the right to take the latter's place."[21]

Again, does today's third position fascism sound more radical than that? Not hardly.

It wasn't just that the early fascists ran under false colors. There was a new militant energy created on the Right by playing "left" off the increasingly stale, dishonest, reformist leanings of organized

socialism. Remember that fascism is a movement of
the young, and that in Italy it was the fascists not the
left that swept the universities with their subculture
of dangerous excitement and drama. As Mussolini
thundered:

> *"... democracy has taken away the sense of style from the
> life of the people. Fascism brings back a sense of style
> to the life of the people, that is, a line of conduct, colour,
> force, the picturesque, the unexpected, the mystic; in short,
> all those things that count in the spirit of the masses. We
> play the lyre on all its strings: from violence to religion,
> from art to politics ... fascism is a desire for action, and **is**
> action; it is not party but anti-party and movement."*[22]

In an unpublished manuscript, R. Vacirca explains
this:

> "Italian Fascism initially positioned itself to the
> *left* of the Social Democracy, denouncing the
> bourgeoisifaction of the socialist movement.
> Mussolini and other early proto-fascists like the
> famous futurist artist Marinelli did this, attract-
> ing many radical youth to them as a more radi-
> cal alternative to the mainstream Marxists. This
> is why Antonio Gramsci and other student social-
> ists idolized Mussolini until he became pro-war
> in 1914. The bourgeois reformist character of the
> Social-Democracy played into the fascists' hands.
> People in the U.S. have a false picture of the his-
> toric euro-left, they don't realize how big and
> strong rooted Social Democracy was. How, like
> our AFL-CIO, the Civil Rights movement, the
> women's movement here, how much a part of the

establishment it had become. And of course from its beginnings fascism was a fighting force, an armed organization. It emphasized violence and direct, spontaneous action which made them look a lot racier than the broad socialist movement which was de facto pacifist. Just like today the 'anti-war movement' Mussolini faced was totally inept and bourgeoisified.

"Up to December of 1920 when the fascists opened up their first big sustained terror campaign against the socialist party, Mussolini presented himself and the fascists as a revolutionary, pro-worker alternative to the increasingly reformist Marxists. Trafficking on his rep as the leader of the most revolutionary faction of the Italian Socialist Party. After all, if he hadn't broken rightward to make common cause with the nationalists and supported Italy entering World War I to gain more territory, Mussolini would have been the natural leader of a communist revolution in Italy. This is what Lenin himself said at one point! This is how disorienting the new fascist movement was. By the time enough people had figured out what Mussolini was doing he had a lock on power, and gradually washed all the red out of his program."[23]

The "classical" fascism openly despised & promised to supplant the bourgeois culture of accumulating capital to live off of, the central fixation with money and soft living. **The Nazi cultural model was not a businessman or politician, remember, but the Aryan warrior willing to fight & kill.** Fascism was a movement for failed men: of the marginally employed professional, the idle school graduate, the deeply indebted farmer, the unrecognized war veteran, the perpetually unemployed worker with no chance of work. But failed not because of *themselves*, but because bourgeois society had failed them in a dishonorable way.

So fascism called men from the middle classes to recover their heritage of being holy warriors, to sweep the decayed old bourgeois order away in a campaign against two classes: to seize State power from the bourgeoisie and completely eliminate the working class left. The bourgeoisie would be forced to step back, would fulfill their useful role in the economy and be rewarded as is needful for capitalism to function, but they could no longer control the State or nation. And the State would be made up of real men who wouldn't profit from the petty counting of stocks, but by manfully just taking what they wanted.

This is the truly rightist revolutionary aspect to fascism, as Hamerquist recognizes. **It is capitalism run out of control of the big capitalists.** Which is why the commanding elements of the capitalist class feed fascism and use it in emergencies, but eventually must try to limit, co-opt, regularize or militarily subdue fascist states. This new World War by the u.s.a. against pan-islamic fascism cannot possibly be more violent than the last world war of the imperialist Allies against European & Japanese fascism — in which 60 million people died. What is the attack on the World Trade Center or the recent bombing of Kabul compared to just the one Allied firebombing of the German city of Dresden? An unknown number of persons in the many tens or even several hundreds of thousands died that night as the uncontrolled firestorm from u.s. "anti-Nazi" bombing sucked the oxygen out of the air and swept through whole city blocks in a leap.

and demolished the building.

What Robert Mathews did will remain forever incomprehensible to many White Americans. How can the average "yuppy," steeped in the values of the "me" generation, understand Mathews' concern for the type of world his son would inherit?

How can the clever lawyer in his $500 suit, accustomed to figuring all the angles before making a move, fathom the soul of someone who knew that he *must* act, regardless of the personal consequences, because it was his responsibility as a man to do so?

How can America's soft, feminized, materialistic masses have any idea of the thinking of a man who made a deliberate choice to die, when he might have lived — to die fearlessly and defiantly — solely so that his death could set an example for other fearless and defiant fighters who would follow him in the years and decades to come?

No, many Americans will not understand. But some will. And they will also understand that in the final showdown there will be no other way but Robert Mathews' way.

No combination of clever lawyers, yuppies, and Joe Sixpacks will ever beat the Jews. Money will not beat them. Brains alone will not beat

William Pierce's National Vanguard (Jan.–Feb. 1985) on Robert Matthews, martyr to modern U.S. nazi movement: a revolutionary movement of real men.

BIG BUSINESS
DID NOT RUN THE FASCIST STATE

Much of the standard old left analysis of the Hitler regime as essentially acting for big business is based on a vulgar Marxism, and is a fundamental misreading of fascism's character. This pseudo-materialist line of thinking says: the biggest German corporations got bigger and richer, so the big capitalists must have been running the show. How simple politics is to those bound and determined to be simple-minded. While Nazism could be thought a "tool" of the bourgeoisie in the sense that big business took advantage of it and supported it, it was out of their control—in other words, not a "tool" in the usual meaning of the word. Picture a type of power saw that you hoped would cut down the tree stump in your backyard, but that not only did that but also went off in its own directions and escaped your control.

There *was* a considerable consolidation of German industry under Nazism, particularly once the war was at its peak. Many small factories were ruthlessly taken from their owners by the Nazi state and given, in effect, to the largest corporations. The fascist interest was in greater ease of government supervision and in spreading the higher state of war production techniques of the advanced corporations.

That this completely contradicted Hitler's "socialist" doctrine of "anti-capitalism" and preserving the small producers, was so evident that even in wartime the Nazis had to politically defend themselves to the public. Notice that even as late as 1943 the Nazis were maintaining the desirability of "socialism" and "anti-capitalism" even as they said it was impractical in the current situation. The *Deutsche Allgeine Zeitung* said in June 1943:

> "It cannot be denied that in practical life things can work out very differently from the ideal National Socialist economy. We find it hard to reconcile ourselves to increasing mechanization ... to the growth of enormous companies, to the decimation of the middle classes which the war has brought about ... But that is the way it is; it would be folly to go counter to technical progress ... Many an old entrenched doctrine of anti-capitalism, with the feelings it engendered, has had to be thrown overboard ... Things are in a state of flux. We should not dread economic concentration."[24]

Hitler being welcomed to the Krupp mansion.

The key misreading is to assume that who made the most profits from business meant anything to Hitler, who personally never cared anything about money and politically hated the bourgeoisie. Wartime focus on productivity aside, Hitler routinely bribed important power elites that he needed to count on. His favorite generals were given whole estates. Even the Prussian aristocracy, whom Hitler personally had contempt for as a decadent elite that had betrayed him in World War I, were given properties as bribes and permitted to rise to high offices in the S.S. In 1942, Prince Salm-Salm was given thirteen mines; Count Asseburg-Falkenstein-Rothkirch got nine silver, mercury, copper, zinc, manganese, lead, iron and sulphur mines; Prince Botho zu Stollberg-Wernigerode received five coal mines, and thirty-nine other mines; etc.[25] The big capitalists, the Krupps, the Flicks, I.G. Farben, General Electric and Ford, obviously profited most of all dollar-wise. But Hitler and the other fascists never gave away any of what mattered to them, control of the State that controlled everything.

To Hitler these bribes were of no more importance than candy passed out to pacify children. As he was reported to have said: **"Why need we trouble to socialize banks and factories? We socialize human beings."**[26]

The previous old left theory that fascism is "a tool of the ruling class," that the capitalists were in effect just faxing their orders in to obedient Adolf every morning, only shows how threadbare left theory had become. Now, generations later, there is no historical evidence that the big German industrial and finance capitalists were dictating Nazi policy on suicidally invading the Soviet Union. Or on putting major efforts into exterminating millions of Jews even at the critical height of the war effort. Or on allying with fascist Japan in an enlarged war bringing the u.s. empire into the conflict. Or the Nazi policy of rigidly dismantling all the conservative lay organizations of the Catholic Church (nonpolitical Catholic women who tried to secretly keep meeting ended up in prisons and concentration camps). And so on.

Hitler even gave early warning that new men remade into Aryan warriors, from classes betrayed by the hated bourgeoisie, would take command of the State to save national capitalist society from the twin evils of the inept capitalists and the left. Fascism, Hitler said, was not another electoral party but a party of warriors who intended to make "revolution":

"On February 24, 1920, the first great public demonstration of our young movement took place. In the Festsaal of the Munich Hofbrauhaus the twenty-five theses of the new party's program were submitted to a crowd of almost two thousand and every single point was accepted amidst jubilant approval.

"With this the first guiding principles and directives were issued for a struggle which was to do away with a veritable mass of old traditional conceptions and opinions and with unclear, yes, harmful aims. Into the rotten and cowardly bourgeois world and into the triumphant march of the Marxist wave of conquest a new power phenomenon was entering, which at the eleventh hour would halt the chariot of doom.

"It was self-evident that the new movement could hope to achieve the necessary importance and the required strength for this gigantic struggle only if it succeeded from the very first day in arousing in the hearts of its supporters the holy conviction that with it political life was to be given, not to a new *election slogan*, but to a new *philosophy* of fundamental significance …

"… And so, if today our movement gets the witty reproach that it is working toward a *'revolution'*, especially from the so-called national bourgeois ministers, say of the Bavarian Center, the only answer we can give one of the political twerps is this: Yes, indeed, we are trying to make up for what you in your criminal stupidity failed to do. By the principles of your parliamentary cattle-trading, you helped to drag the nation into the abyss; but we, in the form of attack and by setting up a new philosophy of life by fanatically and indomitably defending its principles, shall build for our people the steps on which it will some day climb back into the temple of freedom.

"And so, in the founding period of our movement, our first concern had always to be directed towards preventing the host of warriors for an exalted conviction from becoming a mere club for the advancement of parliamentary interests."[27]

The nature of the capitalist State and how it operates *is* a complex issue. For example, it has not been unusual for the capitalist State to actually be operated by another class. In Great Britain, the

feudal State had been administered by the hereditary landed aristocracy, who simply continued to
run the government for well over the first century
of British industrial capitalism. That was particularly
true for the imperial military, traditionally officered
by the younger sons of the aristocracy and gentry.
Germany had a similar arrangement until the end of
World War I, with the military in particular being the
domain of the junkers and other aristocrats (Prince
Otto von Bismarck, the brilliant founder of the modern German capitalist nation, was himself a noble not
a capitalist politician). So in that sense the concept of
fascism commanding the State, relegating the capitalist class to the temporary role of passengers not
drivers in their own car, is not completely without
historical precedent.

A NEW BARBARISM?

Fascism & Anti-Fascism raises the possibility of fascist revolution leading to a de-civilization, of a post-
capitalist regression into a new "barbarism." As
Hamerquist writes insightfully: *"Capitalism's current
contradictions provide the potentials for revolutionary fascist
movements, the basic ingredient, I think, of 'barbarism', just
as certainly as they provide potentials for a revitalized revolutionary left."*

He might well be right. Although, again, plain
vanilla fascism seems to be capable of almost as much

barbarism as human society can absorb (if we consider the case of the Khmer Rouge, it might be that
such extreme breakdown into a neo-barbarism could
come from the authoritarian left more than the right).
When we say that one automatically thinks of the
Holocaust, but the "classical" fascism did much more
than that alone. Hamerquist notes that while capitalism is supposed to live off of the exploitation of
labor power fascism raises the possibility of a "barbaric" mode of surplus value extraction that rests on
the actual *destruction* of labor power. This is a terrible
thing, but it is not new for capitalism. For that matter,
"classical" very capitalist German fascism did exactly
that. It dissolved the German proletariat as a class,
drafting it into their army or promoting it away, and
created a better, disposable, always-dying-off working class that was literally being worked to death.

Even political conquest didn't eliminate National
Socialism's constant clashing with their own native
industrial working class. As the Party's German
Labor Front reported in 1937 over mass resistance to
speed-ups and Taylorism: "*Workers, whether of National
Socialist persuasion or not, still hold on to the Marxist and
union position of rejecting critera of production ... Controls
over individual achievement are rejected. Therefore they
resist all attempts to time them.*"[28] Remember that until
well after 1933 the Nazis could venture into hard-
core proletarian neighborhoods only in large groups.
There were large-scale working class sabotage campaigns in the shipyards, docks, railroads and armaments factories (Italian fascism was always plagued
by strong working class opposition, and was basically overthrown by the Italian workers).

Fascism de-proletarianized Aryan society. Or to put it more precisely: it *created* an Aryan society that had never existed before by de-proletarianizing and genociding the former German society. The Nazis pursued Adolf Hitler's evolving strategy, which was to simultaneously promote both techno-industrial development and the Aryan re-organization of classes. If it is the superior race man's destiny to be both a fierce soldier and ruler over others—as the Nazis held in a core belief—then how can this superior race man at the same time be packing groceries for housewives at the supermarket or bucking production on the assembly line? In 1940 Nazi Labor Front leader Robert Ley said in an amazingly revealing speech: *"In ten years Germany will be transformed beyond recognition. A nation of proletarians will have become a nation of rulers..."* By the millions, newly Aryanized men were shifted into military & police service and into being supervisors, office workers, foremen,

Nazi propaganda poster from Austria, 1942: "We Women Know Our Duty."

straw bosses and minor bureaucrats of every sort. The new proletariat that started emerging was heavily made up of involuntary foreign & slave laborers, retirees, and—despite Nazi ideology about women's "natural" place in the kitchen and nursery—women.[29]

Nazi slave labor is seldom dealt with in its class reality. Usually it is mentioned as a side-effect of the Holocaust. Or as a short-lived desperation measure of a tottering regime facing military defeat on all fronts. The truth was that it was much more than that. Slave and semi-slave labor was a necessary feature of mature Nazi society. If Hitlerism had been successful, slave labor was to have gone on for his entire lifetime and beyond. Even conquered Eastern Europe and Russia, in official Nazi plans, would gradually have given way to the spread of vast Aryan owned agricultural estates, whose rural slave proletariat would have been involuntarily furnished by the inferior races.[30]

By 1941 there were three million foreign & slave proletarians at work in National Socialist factories, farms and mines. Coincidentally, the Nazi elite S.S.—which had only 116 men at its first public display at the July 4, 1926 Party Rally at Weimar[31] (by happy coincidence the u.s.a. and the Nazi Party celebrate the same founding holiday)—had symmetrically grown to three million as well. A new class of oppressed workers being balanced by a new class of parasitic oppressors. Soon the overrun territories of Europe and the East provided over four million more slave laborers for Nazi industry & the war machine (the majority of whom were used up, consumed, in accelerated capitalist production). Nazism's peculiar class structure was parasitic as a mode of life. One history sums this up:

> "The regime's increasing use of concentration camp and foreign forced labour made the working class more or less passive accomplices in Nazi racial policy ... The first 'recruits' were unemployed Polish agricultural labourers, who were soon accompanied by prisoners of war and people abducted en masse from cinemas and churches. These were then followed by the French. By the summer of 1941 there were some three million foreign workers in Germany, a figure which mushroomed to 7.7 million in the autumn of 1944. ... *A high proportion of these workers were either young or female.* By 1944, a quarter of those working in the German economy were foreigners. Virtually every German worker was thus confronted by the fact and practice of Nazi racism. In some branches of industry, German workers merely constituted a thin, supervisory layer above a workforce of which between 80 and 90 percent were foreigners. This tends to be passed over by historians of the labour movement.
>
> "Treatment of these foreign workers was largely determined by their 'racial' origins. Broadly speaking, the usual hierarchy consisted of 'German workers' at the top, 'west workers' a stage below them, and Poles and 'eastern workers' at the lowest level. This racial hierarchy determined both living conditions and the degree of coercion to which foreign workers were

subjected both at the workplace and in society at large."[32]

The dis-visionary fascist social engineering of the Nazi Party several generations ago is echoed by the pan-islamic fascists of the Taliban, who ordered the permanent house arrest and enslavement of all women in society as a gender (as well as the marginalization/elimination of other ethnic groupings). Fascism as we have known it in practice, operating as an "extraordinary" form of capitalist rule, produces shocking barbarism far beyond any normal expectations. In fact, to go much beyond that in this direction would probably produce an unraveling of society itself (as happened under the Khmer Rouge).

FASCIST SUCCESS
& THE CAPITALIST STATE

Although the major bourgeoisie itself is not needed to create fascist movements, neither is it true that fascism simply comes in cold from the outside to seize State power. It is *not* like the revolutionary left in that sense. We feel that revolutionaries must make a critical distinction between the various sectors of the capitalist class and the State apparatus that protects capitalism. Fascism has a certain insider leverage in its reaching for State power. In all cases of fascist success so far there has been a complex mutual attraction between elements of the State and fascist movements. Fascism gets important support from operators within the bourgeois State, who recognize their deepest identities and needs in these popular movements of the extreme right. *"Like is drawn to like."*

Big businessmen, the hereditary super-wealthy, financiers, are notoriously inept at State decision-making. The capitalist State cannot necessarily survive crises by being bound to their thinking (recall the widespread capitalist opposition to Franklin Roosevelt and the New Deal, even to the point of an attempted military coup led by the DuPonts). President Theodore Roosevelt once remarked on this with disappointment: *"You expect a man of millions to be a man worth hearing. But as a rule they don't know anything outside their own businesses."*[33]

The infant Nazi Party, for example, might have had no support at all from the big bourgeoisie, but it was carefully fostered for years by elements in the young army officer corps. This was at a time, right after Germany's defeat in World War I, when the German army was politically unreliable from the capitalist point of view. To ensure that some officers didn't try a coup to oust the new social-democratic Weimar Republic government, the enlisted men in many army units had elected socialist representatives to meet in councils. Rebellious army units went socialist or even communist.

Professional officers knew that without a mass base of support, a "workers party" as one captain in the Bavarian regiments put it, they wouldn't be able to repress the rebellious working class left or trust their own troops enough to stage the coup they aimed for. This particular officer had spotted a likely political worker for their conspiracy in his battalion, a corporal named Adolf Hitler who had successfully become the elected socialist representative of his company. This corporal was quickly recruited to be a political agent for the rightist officers conspiracy in the army.

Hitler later said in awkwardly defending Nazis with socialist pasts: *"Everyone was a social-democrat once."* The lesson here is that it's not uncommon in the chaos when regimes fall, when radical discontent is the major drum beat of popular politics, for even rightists to get their early political experience by joining the left for awhile. Sometimes that's the best game in town. Hitler's biographer, Ian Kershaw, points out that the young corporal was far more heavily involved in the left than was earlier realized. Bavaria in South Germany went from overthrowing both the Kaiser and its own principality all the way to its own "Red Republic" when the young communists seized power temporarily. Hitler's 1st Reserve Battalion of the 2nd Bavarian Infantry Regiment took part in the communist revolution, during which he served as the elected Deputy Battalion Representative, probably even marching in an armed workers & soldiers parade wearing a red armband with the rest of his unit.[34]

In this he was far from being the only fascist-to-be drawn into rebellious "socialist" activity. The commander of his elite S.S. bodyguard, Sepp Dietrich (later to become an S.S. General and war criminal), had first been the elected chairman of a revolutionary soldiers' council in 1919. Hitler's own chauffeur, Julius Schreck, had been in the communist "Red Army" militia, while his first propaganda chief, Herman Esser, had been a socialist journalist. These were men looking for a cause, for change that they could swell into, and with an anger at the smug bourgeoisie.[35] The left after all teaches how to conduct political debates, how to organize masses of people around issues, the technique of mass politics.

When the unsuccessful Kapp Putsch broke out in Berlin in 1920, political agent Hitler was even trusted enough to be sent secretly to be the liaison between the Bavarian army units and the mutinous officers.[36] By then a full time army political specialist, Hitler was sent undercover to join and report on a small fascist group called the German National Socialist Workers Party (one of many promising rightist and fascist groups the army was encouraging). Hitler had finally found his life's work, and with army approval and financing Hitler plunged into building the Nazi Party. He was one of many such competing agents, in those chaotic times. The German Army acted autonomously from the rest of the weakened bourgeois democratic State for years, illegally giving the Nazi Party and other far right groups funds, weapons and training.

While there are rogue operations and unofficially approved assistance to fascists, there are also cases where the State on all levels gets involved. Italy was one such case, where the newborn fascist movement in 1919–22 got informal local help from police and army officers as well as official assistance from the highest levels of the State. Arrested with a hundred other fascists after the 1919 elections on charges of flashing guns (Mussolini lost to a socialist candidate by 40 to 1), Mussolini was freed on government orders.[36] In 1920, the defense minister ordered that demobilized officers who joined the fascist action squads to give leadership to the mix of inexperienced middle class students and street criminals in them would continue to get four fifths of their army pay.[37] But it wasn't the Italian big bourgeoisie who were so enthusiastic about supporting fascism but police officials, army officers, local capitalists and the rural middle class landowners and intellectuals. It wasn't until the eve of the fascist march on Rome in 1922, when Mussolini was being supported by the heads of the military for the next chief of state, that the major industrial capitalists swung into line.[38]

We can see this pattern over and over on all levels. *Because the potential usefulness of mass volunteer movements of armed men is irresistible to those in the State who actually have to solve capitalism's crises.* **(Many within the State apparatus naturally have**

approximate fascist or "totalitarian" views themselves.) And today these mass volunteer movements of armed men are equally irresistible to the small and local bourgeoisie, who feel increasingly neglected by and estranged from the command levels of big transnational capitalism.

Afghanistan and pan-islamic fascism in that region today are a more recent development that shows how this type of relationship can play out. It is certainly true that the fascist Taliban movement is a byproduct of the Reagan administration's manufactured islamic jihad, in the sense that the c.i.a. set the historical stage for the Taliban to appear. But the fascist movement known as the Taliban ("the Students") was primarily an internal development of Pakistani-Afghan society.[39]

Pakistani military dictator General Zia took that c.i.a. strategy and ran with it in a strategy of his own, to deliberately create out of the refugee camps and Pakistan's dispossessed a huge manipulated guerrilla army of jihad. General Zia's decision is cursed by many in Pakistan today, but it made sense in terms of his class situation. The Pakistani bourgeois officer class was locked into a bitter cycle of losing conflicts with their main enemy, India, which is far larger and stronger. While the cramped, neo-colonial Pakistani economy is in continual crisis, with ever more bitter misery and class conflict.

General Zia envisioned giving Pakistan "strategic depth," enlarging it economically and militarily by making Pakistan the center and leadership of a new transnational Muslim empire styled after the historic Muslim Central Asian empire of the

Tartars. Uniting Afghanistan, Uzbekistan, Tajikistan, Turkmenistan, Muslim China, Kashmir and the 150 million Muslims of India itself, with Pakistan as the center. The mujaheddin were to be the Brownshirts, the "Stormtroopers," the mass popular armed force, acting for the Pakistani army and local bourgeoisie.

When "liberated" Afghanistan disintegrated into mujaheddin looting, mass rapes, killings and ethnic civil war so characteristic of men's religions, the Taliban became the Pakistan state's fix-it to unify and hold down the country. Their sponsor was Lt-General Hameed Gul, the c.i.a.'s former chief collaborator in their Afghan operation as head of the feared Pakistan Inter Service Intelligence (ISI). He was the leader overseeing the funding, training and

arming of all the various mujaheddin groups, and subsequently became the Taliban's main sponsor. Providing arms, intelligence and military "advisors" to them.

The Taliban was financially supported by the large Pakistani smuggling mafias (which they became part of). That is, the Taliban leaders are little local bourgeoisie themselves, but of a special criminal kind. Because of its central location and long borders in rough terrain, Afghanistan has always been a hub where commercial traffic goes from Pakistan and its ports across the borders into Iran or China and up into the former USSR via Turkmenistan, Uzbekistan and Tajikistan. And back. We're talking about many hundreds of trucks a day loaded with televisions, computers, silk clothing, food, diesel fuel, rifles and ammunition, and especially drugs. All smuggled, and usually on stolen trucks. Again, a corrosive trade worth billions of dollars a year.

The smuggling mafias are certainly businessmen, but what we'd call small local capitalists. They don't care too much for NATO, the UN, the multinational corporations and the WTO, for obvious reasons. What they do care about is having a stable corrupt police over Afghanistan's highways. During the free-for-all period right after the pro-Russian Kabul government fell in 1992 and before the Taliban took over in 1995–96, each local warlord and his gunmen set up roadblocks. A long truck convoy might be "taxed" dozens of times. Violent chaos is bad for real crime.

So the Pakistani smuggling mafias started not only backing the Taliban financially and politically, but helping them join the business. The Taliban, a new fascist movement of Pashtun nationalism, led thousands of fresh but inexperienced fighters in a new jihad to unify all the armies and end the fighting. Like a miracle, the Taliban marched on the capital and beyond, sweeping armies before them by the simple expedient of buying the loyalty of warlord commanders with cash supplied by their mafia backers. Their forces swelled as they incorporated old warlord forces into their new army of Pashtun unity, as well as being joined by some 20,000 enthusiastic new recruits from the refugee camps in Pakistan. This is the clerical fascist military regime that came to temporarily rule Afghanistan.

There is widespread class antagonism towards the big transnational bourgeoisie of Western imperialism among Muslim local capitalists and the mafias of criminal capitalism, who see no advantage to their own classes in having the big transnational corporations take over even the smallest corners of the Third World. While modern society in the Muslim world keeps turning out large numbers of declassed, educated and semi-educated young men who have no prospects in their countries. And there are elements in the neo-colonial State apparatus who see in fascism the best solution for their class and social crises. Like Lt-General Gul, formerly the c.i.a.'s "man in Afghanistan."

Lt-General Gul himself is now widely considered a supporter or member of the pan-islamic fascist network. Since helping the Taliban into power Gul has broken with the c.i.a. and the big imperialist bourgeoisie. Now having left the army, General Gul is making well-received speeches against the pro-Western Pakistani military regime, calling the u.s. bombing of Afghanistan part of the *"Zionist conspiracy"* that he alleges did 911. The Trade attack, this former major c.i.a. ally says, was merely a staged Jewish *"pretext for a long-prepared, all-out operation … for subjugation of the Muslim world. Jihad has, therefore, become obligatory on all Muslims, wherever they are."*[40] You can imagine the public ripple effect of having Pakistan's connection to the c.i.a. making anti-Western imperialist speeches like this.

The point is that fascism never has to fight alone. Why should it? Since along that road, in the deepening crisis and tumult of transformation, it attracts significant involvement from local or small bourgeoisie and elements of the State apparatus. Whether covert or open, rogue or official. We should see that in fascism now some of the local bourgeoisie, declassed masses of men, criminal elements and part of the State apparatus come together in a new way.

TRENDS TOWARD UNEXPECTED FASCIST INFECTIONS?

One of *Fascism & Anti-Fascism*'s conclusions is that the left and the fascists are competing for the same people, especially in the white working class. While this can be questioned, one place this could be most dangerously true is in the Black Nation. Hamerquist's analysis here is controversial. Even the thought of any Black fascism sounds strange, since the traditional humanism of Black politics and any fascism have always been at opposite poles from each other. But in the 21st century everything is transforming. We already have seen a Chicano nationalist website that defends the *Protocols of the Elders of Zion*, the most important single propaganda writing for world fascism. As well as a Chicano community newspaper in Los Angeles that has similar politics.

No nation in the world has undergone more radical change in the last generation than the New Afrikan Nation. The previous New Afrikan society was a semi-colonial one, where a stable Black working class played a central role both in its community and in u.s. industrial production. The democratic and humanist politics that we associate with Black culture were due not only to that Black working class culture but to the unusually democratic gender relationships, with Black women having a power among their own that euro-amerikan women have never known.

A continuing wave of integration has reshaped the class structure and culture. While integration on a social level never happened (or was greatly desired by anyone), integration of middle class employment has created a large New Afrikan middle class. Counter-balancing that has been the squeezing of the traditional New Afrikan working class, which has seen its unionized industrial jobs disappear overseas while much of the New Afrikan lower working class has been displaced by Latino emigrant labor. The class nature of the poor has changed, from lower working class to large numbers of declassed, in particular declassed men.

This has been the setting for the rise of authoritarian male institutions in the old core New Afrikan communities. These authoritarian organizations and subcultures have rightist politics, and are unprecedented in the New Afrikan Nation's history. We have already seen the rise of various Black rightist-nationalist figures with a mass following, most notably the late Khalid Muhammad. And the regularization of what were once youth gangs, but now are sometimes Black paramilitary mafias with even thousands of soldiers and many millions of dollars in revenues. Who are de facto "Bantustan" subcontractors of the u.s. empire, policing and perhaps semi-governing small territories where poor communities of New Afrikans live. All against the related background of amoral cultural trends where the obsessive gathering of luxuries and violent preying of Black on Black is celebrated.

This is a shock amidst the almost seismic changes in all of the u.s. empire as it sheds its old continental form and becomes a globalized society. It is hard to know at this moment what will eventually result. To illustrate with but one example, post-911 the old New Afrikan struggle against police repression and racist brutality was temporarily thrown off balance by sweeping security checks of everyone, as well as widespread "ethnic profiling" in which Black people were for the first time not the designated enemy but among those expected to do the profiling.

Hamerquist starts by pointing out that new white fascist groups might well find *"working relationships and alliances"* with *"various nationalist and religious tendencies among oppressed peoples."* Here Hamerquist puts his finger on one of the strangest and least explored aspects of Black nationalism. That there is such a pattern of occasional ties to white far rightists.

The most powerful Black nationalist organization in u.s. history, the Honorable Elijah Muhammad's Nation of Islam in the 1960s, definitely had relations with various white far right and fascist groups. This was public knowledge. Malcolm X himself said that he had been directed by the NOI leader to meet with Ku Klux Klan men to accept financial contributions. One article on the NOI noted that:

> "…in 1961 at a NOI rally in Washington, DC, American Nazi George Lincoln Rockwell sat in the front row with a few dozen storm troopers. When it came time for the collection, Rockwell cried out: *'George Lincoln Rockwell gives $20.'* So much applause followed that Malcolm X remarked, *'George Lincoln Rockwell, you got the biggest hand you ever got, didn't you?'* In 1962, at the NOI's annual Savior's Day in Chicago, Rockwell was a featured speaker. He stated, *'I believe Elijah Muhammad is the Adolph Hitler of the Black man,'* and ended his speech by pumping his arm and shouting, *'Heil Hitler'.* "

It isn't hard in retrospect to see what Rockwell was up to. At a time when Freedom struggles were sweeping the u.s., when u.s. capitalism was defensively promoting integration, some white fascists like Rockwell pushed the line that a program of racial separatism had considerable support from militant Black leaders.

On his part, the Honorable Elijah Muhammad might have viewed Rockwell's visits as a public lesson: that even those whites who thought the least of Black people were recognizing the Nation of Islam as a power to be respected (to say that such a viewpoint was at best very narrow is an understatement). As early as the 1920s, during the rise of the Ku Klux Klan to the status of a mass nationwide organization of millions, there was a tentative but well-publicized alliance between the KKK and Black Pan-Afrikanist leader Marcus Garvey. There again, the link was a common interest in promoting the idea of national separatism (although the two sides meant very different things by it).

All these were rare episodes, marginal propaganda events as opposed to any actual alliance. So clearly out of step with the humanist beliefs of the New Afrikan people that they quickly passed away into the history books. **But since then a major development has rearanged the New Afrikan political landscape. For the first time, major authoritarian trends have manifested themselves *within* the Black community.**

We are used to thinking of national liberation movements as being pro-freedom, of being a force for liberation. **But all nationalist movements have inherently *both* liberating and repressive possibilities, based on different class politics within a broad mass movement.** It would be a mistake, for instance, to view the historic Nation of Islam as just being around the politics of Malcolm X. He gradually became a radical anti-capitalist, as he himself said many times. He wasn't a "Marxist" or an "anarchist" in a European ideological framework, but identified with the communal socialist ideas that had grown within many anti-colonial revolutions. Malcolm's Black nationalism was a nationalism of the oppressed classes, which is to say it was *internationalist* at its heart. When he famously cried out, "The Black Revolution is sweeping Asia! The Black Revolution is sweeping Latin America! The Black Revolution is sweeping Africa!", it was obvious that to him it wasn't about a race or a nation but about the world's oppressed majority. And he lived what he said. While it was the practice for the NOI to operate as a franchised business, with the local minister being given property and the right to keep all the revenues raised above the quotas assigned by Chicago, Malcolm refused to accept personal wealth.

It is always said that Malcolm's distinction was that he was the hardest on white people. Which is the kind of falsehood that the oppressor culture likes to slyly perpetuate. No, violently denouncing obvious white racism is so easy that anyone can do it & just turn up the volume. His distinction was that he was unrelentingly, harshly truthful about his own people and their situation. For a generation Malcolm was the teacher. When the Los Angeles police invaded the mosque there one night in 1962, the Fruit of Islam security guards fought them at the entrance to uphold the NOI's policy barring the oppressor. Police gunfire killed one man and wounded many others. As criminal trials and national headlines grew, Malcolm X gave a fiery press conference at the mosque with one of the wounded brothers, paralyzed in a wheelchair. After accusing the police of being the only criminals and instigators, Malcolm rebuked the Fruit of Islam. They had fallen down on their oath, he reminded them. The oppressor should enter the mosque only if its defenders were all slain. Resistance to the full, without holding anything back, was necessary for the freedom of their people (soon after that, police departments all over the country, including Los Angeles and New York, quietly ordered that no units attempt to enter a mosque without permission of the minister).

In contrast, some other NOI ministers pursued the development of their church as a business opportunity while helping the u.s. government in the programmed assassination of Malcolm — all covered up by polished anti-u.s. speechmaking. In effect, the pro-capitalist wing of the Nation of Islam became a "loyal opposition" to America. In return, they were allowed to exploit Black people as much as they could. In at least three cities after Malcolm's death, ministers used the mosque and the Fruit of Islam in the drug trade with cooperation from the police. A certain pattern was established, where the u.s. government and police protect and even financially support right-wing Black nationalists who used a pseudo-militance towards White America to build followings.

We have to grasp the fuller pattern. These rightists were not an outright puppet for white interests such as a Clarence Thomas is (although right-wing Black nationalists publicly supported Thomas's Supreme Court nomination in their role as a "loyal opposition"). Their class position is much more complex than that. They are bourgeois nationalists, believing in the salvation of their Race through the rise of a commanding bourgeoisie and its industries. In other words, instead of working for white corporations the Black Man should build his own, as every major capitalist nation had done. The reason that all capitalism has historically been nationalistic is that to rise from nothing, a bourgeoisie needs to start by having its very own people to exploit (how can you exploit other nations if you haven't built some strength by sucking on your own people first?). Most importantly, you need to disempower and oppress women as a gender, to break up the communal culture that is the barrier to capitalist accumulation. And deals and cooperation with more powerful rivals are just business sense to bourgeois nationalism, as when Minister Louis Farrakhan "explained" the divine revelation that Allah chose Malcolm for death as a warning to the Black faithful not to directly oppose the u.s. government (so the f.b.i./c.i.a. and Minister Farrakhan himself get off for killing Malcolm X, while poor old Allah has to take the rap).

The defeat of New Afrikan revolutionary nationalism after the mass uprisings of the 1960s opened the way for new developments, including a nationalism dominated by rightist politics. These new authoritarian trends manifested themselves most clearly in the rise of male institutions unprecedented in the Black Nation's history. Led by the breakout of Black women, more and more New Afrikans reject a nationalist separatism that would only produce a *more* repressed life than they already had under u.s. capitalism.

But the struggle of oppressed peoples for liberation not only always rises and ebbs, but always takes many new forms. It meets change with change, with rethinking & mass creativity. The 1960s Black Revolution changed the world but then was defeated. But that same spirit and energy reemerged in new people, sidestepped into new cultural fronts. The fight for political awareness vs. misogyny and amoralism in hip hop and poetry slams is only the most obvious example. Davey D, talking about last April's rap concert to raise funds for Jamil Al-Amin's defense, reminded young rappers how the new has many different roots in the old radicalism:

> "In the meantime it is only fitting that the Hip Hop community has come out in force to aid Al-Amin. While he is best known for all the work he put in for the Civil Rights struggle, for many H Rap Brown had a profound yet unintended connection to Hip Hop. In his autobiography Die Nigger Die H Rap talked about his life and the things he did as a kid growing up. Among the things he spends a considerable time talking about, was the verbal rhyme games he played as a kid. H Rap got his name because he had a gift for gab. In his book he showed that he was a master rhymer, 30 years before Hip Hop made its way to the Bronx. He participated in all sorts of verbal games ranging from Signifying to The Dozens.

> "As quiet as kept, many of the early rhymes used by Hip Hoppers … can be found in H Rap's book. In his book he talks about the huge circles people would form when rhyming against each other. Sometimes there would be as many as 30–40 people verbally sparring each other in a rhyme game known as The Dozens … long before modern day Hip Hop hit the scene cats like H Rap Brown was putting down some serious rhymes. It's a shame to

*see a brother who gave so much to the struggle in this cur-
rent predicament."*

And on the other hand, surely the mass advance of
New Afrikan women by the millions breaking out of
old roles and trampling under old limitations is going
to change the future in ways no one can predict. This
may end up being the biggest grassroots change in
this generation.

Even troubling trends the paper alludes to—like
the hostility to new immigration and immigrant
labor—might be problematic but also are complex
and *not* the same as the familiar "Kill Arabs!" racism
seen after 911 in u.s. society at large. New Afrikans
see very clearly that the new tidal wave of immigrant labor—not just from South Asia and Mexico
but from Poland and China and other places—is not
just accidental but has been encouraged by u.s. capitalism in part as a racist strategy to undermine the
leverage that Black workers had previously gained.

The discussion of internal fascism or other repressive authoritarianisms has been blocked by a number of factors. Such as the strong feeling that any
such problem can only be insignificant, given that
it goes against the historic grain of Black society
(as an example: a group like the Hebrew Israelites
may or may not be fascist, but there are few New
Afrikans interested in joining them today). Or that it
only detracts from the main focus on repression from
White America and its government.

Another factor is the wince at even hearing the
phrase "Black fascism," after decades of Black leaders and militants being denounced as "racists" and

"fascists" by the u.s. government and the zionists. (One 1960s book on world fascism even had a section on Malcolm X.) But the New Afrikan Nation is not back in slavery days, in an oppressed monoclass where there was essentially no political expression on the right. A developed society of 40 millions, the Black Nation has a full spectrum of classes and class politics just as any other nation in the world. It has a far right as well as a left, whether people want to recognize it or not. It certainly has some who are "wickedly great," to use a term coined by one major Black leader, now that capitalist neo-colonialism has opened up startling possibilities never dreamed of before.

Although this is not the place for any real discussion on Black gangs, they have a place in future politics, too. Because they're *all* about politics. Not that a criminal gang per se is a fascist organization, although they can resonate along that line. But in the 1990s the u.s. justice department named one particular Black gang as their "number one" target for national investigation & prosecution. This sounded like a strange choice, unless you know the details. The capitalist media talks about gangs as a crime problem, when really it's not about crime (since they're only killing and destroying the lives of New Afrikans, which isn't a crime to America). Although they are public, large and illegal, few if any Black gangs—such as the Vice-Lords which date back to the 1930s or the El-Rukyns which has neighborhood courts where personal disputes are settled and whose leaders were formally invited to President Nixon's inaugural ball—have been ended by the police. Because Black gangs aren't about youth and aren't about crime, although they do crime. They are new violent institutions informally sanctioned by u.s. capitalism, like death squads or drug cartels are, formed as capitalism adapts to this new zone of protracted crisis.

Like many other gangs, this organization controlled a large territory in which its thousands of armed members essentially ruled streets and de facto much of the lives of the population (while it enrolled thousands of youth, much of its structure and leadership were not only adult but middle-aged). Nothing from selling drugs to anti-racist campaigns could take place without their permission. It made and ran on millions of dollars each year in criminal economics. This was tacitly approved of by the police and government, as a "sterilization" to ensure that mass Black revolt did not sweep the inner cities as in the 1960s. Situation normal. It's not quite Betty Crocker, but it really *is* America as we know it.

However, unlike most gang organizations, it had a leadership with as much practical social-political vision as any George Washington. In the ruthless u.s. counterinsurgency against the 1960s Black liberation movement, their inner city territory had been left a devastated postwar terrain of the type all too familiar to us. A vacuum deliberately maintained by u.s. capitalism. This gang organization decided to fill that vacuum, to become something like an underground dictatorial state. Not only by building illicit ties with policemen and government officials (and sending their own soldiers into the police and correctional guards), not only by starting its own businesses & stores, but by running popular Black anti-racist political campaigns and placing its own electoral candidates in the Democratic Party.

So it wanted to have its own economy and its own share of local State power, as well as violent control of the streets. When it started using indirect federal grants to carry out successful mass voter registration campaigns, with rallies of thousands of people cheering its leading figures, red lights went off. *This possibility of a Black quasi-state inside a major u.s. city pushed all the buttons in Washington.* This gang organization is *not* a fascist party, of course. And neither the organization nor the members have fascist ideology — a mafia is a closer example. But there are fascist precursors in the mass gang subculture. A mass armed criminal organization of declassed men that wants not only to have a rough control of the local population but have a linked economic and political program of domination has taken a step towards fascism (many white criminal gangs are already consciously pro-fascist, of course). Such possible future fascist developments might take a nationalist, "anti-racist" or religious outward form.

From afar, from outside the New Afrikan Nation, it seems that *Fascism & Anti-Fascism*'s analysis in this particular section is too hurriedly done on too little knowledge (a criticism that i doubt the author would disagree with). Still, the contribution here is that the paper opens the door to questions revolutionaries need to deal with. The point the paper is making is that Black fascist infections — small but troubling in the changed light of new authoritarian trends — are an ordinary reality just as in many other nations.[41]

UNANSWERED QUESTIONS

The onrush of events is forcing everyone not only to think about fascism alone. What is most significant about rethinking fascism isn't that the left's traditional view of fascism is outmoded; what's most significant is finding that the left's view of the *world* is outmoded. Assumptions so ingrained that they were never really discussed have been forcefully overturned. As much as we've tried to find new answers instead of just repeating old left slogans, there is no shortage of obvious questions that we haven't answered.

— — — — — — —

No sensible revolutionary is holding their breath expecting some Great Depression to suddenly do a mass organizing job for us. And imperialism shows no signs of collapsing on its own anytime soon. But there *is* some glossed over infection in the blood, something critical happening within the capitalist structures.

Like a positive lab test, the rise of fascism proves that world capitalism's intoxicating moment of historic triumph is not quite as it seems. For it itself is in deep systemic crisis. The system is not working as the big capitalists want it to. *Even within the empire of the affluent European Union, capitalism's very development has led to a twilight zone of protracted crisis that is, on a national level, seemingly beyond either reform or ordinary repression.* Will this come to symbolize the system as a whole?

— — — — — — —

Fascism always had to be imposed by the ruling class, we thought. We assumed that it could never be popular, especially in Europe where it had such a disastrous track record in living memory. Yet fascism and the associated far right now has a surging mass base, and is the "democratic" choice of millions of Europeans. In Austria, known fascist elements are now in the ruling government coalition. It has pushed the whole political spectrum to the right in Europe, as the ruling class is forced to experiment Frankenstein-like with transplanting parts of fascism into the body of European bourgeois democracy.

— — — — — — —

Has fascism become a type of institutionalized subculture, of lifestyle, within world capitalism? Will we see new hybrid capitalist societies, part bourgeois democratic and part fascist as societies splinter into different zones? Just as in Germany now there is a gulf between the cosmopolitan city of Dusseldorf, regional home to Japanese and other transnational corporations, and the "no go" zones of the welfare state German East, where fascists gangs often own the street.

— — — — — — —

Through what mechanisms — practically speaking — do we see the imperialist ruling class directing their national States now that they are also outgrowing them? Is the relationship of classes changing within capitalism? How autonomous can the State be in capitalist society? What is the role of hegemony rather than direct hands-on control in capitalism being maintained?

Although fascism is new historically speaking, we have yet to see a stable fascist regime (in retrospect the Franco regime in Spain was clearly — as the Nazis privately complained — a conservative Catholic dictatorship rather than a fascist one, although there were fascists in it). Is fascist rule only a temporary sterilizing interlude before the big bourgeoisie has to reassert control? Fascism as a State power has at least two obvious destabilizing attributes: By repressing or eliminating sections of society — such as Jewish scientists or educated women — it forecloses much of its own needed competitive development. Since it adds new mass repressive layers of soldiers and administrators who produce nothing & must feed off of an already weakened economy, fascism tends towards aggressive wars, looting, and criminal enterprises which bring it into conflict with other capitalist nation-states. There is an underlying liberal attitude that fascism is so self-defeating that it can be outwaited. What does this mean for us?

— — — — — — —

What is true for the prosperous metropolis is even more true for the Third World, for that part of world capitalism that is the neo-colonial periphery. *Here the zone of protracted crisis cannot be hidden.* How long can this state of seemingly permanent crisis be maintained, unresolved?

A journalist from the *New York Times* recently visited a Pakistani village, to profile the men who had left as jihad volunteers to go fight the u.s. in Afghanistan. One striking information was that none of the young men who went had ever had regular jobs or any future expectation of having them. Once these were the men who might have been recruited by left parties and the national liberation movements, but the world failure of the Marxist left has spotlighted the far right as a hope for social change to many people who simply will not stay as they are.

The assumption that in fighting fascism we would automatically enjoy majority support has crashed — just look at India or Austria right now. As has the delusion that fascism built its movements solely on bigotry and violence. Even the Nazi movement not only strongly manipulated themes of social justice and restoring civic order, but built its mass base by a grassroots network of fighting squads, self-help groups and social services. What fascists did crudely in 1930 is being done in a much more sophisticated

way today—as we can see in the Muslim world. In place after place, the far right is drawing on the energy of "anti-colonialism" and anti-Western imperialism. *This is the more complex rearrangement of the political landscape, the first new political shape of the 21st century.*

And the zone of protracted crisis beyond reform or repression keeps growing, deepening. Here in the metropolis, it is hard even for the politically aware to grasp what this fully means. Here is some local news from just one day, one issue of the respected Karachi, Pakistan daily newspaper *DAWN* (for Thursday October 11, 2001):

- A petty officer assigned to the naval destroyer *PNS Dilawar* was shot dead in his apartment by unidentified assassins who broke his door in and then fled.

- Chairman Syed Hasan of the Sindh Board of Technical Education was killed by assassins on a motorcycle as he was getting into his car.

- *"Under cover of Anti-U.S. protests certain religious extremists seem to be busy settling old scores."* Mobs of men were led to attack the NGOs serving the refugee areas. UNICEF and UNHCR offices in Quetta were burned, and many smaller NGOs were attacked. *DAWN* reports: *"The championing of causes such as human rights, rights of working women, girls schooling and family planning by the NGOs had drawn the ire of religious extremists."*

- Former ISI Chief Lt-General Hameed Gul was invited to address the Lahore High Court Bar Association, where he repeated his call for jihad, and contributions to aid the fascist war effort were gathered from the assembled lawyers and judges.

● The Anti-Terrorist Wing of the Police arrested four members of a "gang," seizing one Kalashnikov assault rifle, three pistols and four hand grenades. The "gang" had assassinated: Hussain Zaidi, Director of Laboratories for the Ministry of Defense; Captain Altar Hussain, divisional engineer of the Pakistan Telephone Company; Dr. Razi Mehdi and Dr. Ishrat Hussan; religious teacher Pesh Imam of Northern Nazimabad.

● Dr. Ayesha Siddiqa-Agha, security analyst, reported that the number of "trained militants" who had gone through rightist military training camps in Pakistan & Afghanistan had doubled in the past fifteen years from one million to two million. She said that the former President Zia's *"deliberate policy of encouraging the growth of militant groups in the country had increased insecurity tenfold."* Just as with the Reagan Administration in the 1980s, the capitalist States seemingly can't stop themselves from making the precise decisions that keep undermining the stability of their own societies.

— — — — — — —

The u.s. response to 911 has rolled out a worldwide display of military power, including levels of domestic surveillance and repression not seen outside of the Black community since the 1901 Anti-Anarchist campaign and the 1920s Red Scare (both, like today's anti-Muslim ethnic profiling, directed officially at immigrants). While this has been characterized by the left as a juggernaut of unchecked State power, it might be just as accurate to term the government repression as a coverup for their increasing weakness. To think of u.s. imperialism as the lone superpower left standing might be expressed differently—as the gradual decline of *all* imperialist nation-state powers. And now only one to go, and it is crumbling not growing stronger. One Chicago position paper after 911 reminded us of this:

> *"Now with this new 'war,' repression is being sold as an acceptable compromise for safety and security … At the same time, the creation of an 'Office of Homeland Security' and this public gloves-off approach to domestic repression shows that 911 has weakened the government even as it puffs itself up in cocky displays of supposed strength. We can't be fooled by this. When they actually have to show force on such a broad scale it means that the usual systems of control have temporarily failed …"*[42]

What are the strategic possibilities for us in this changed situation?

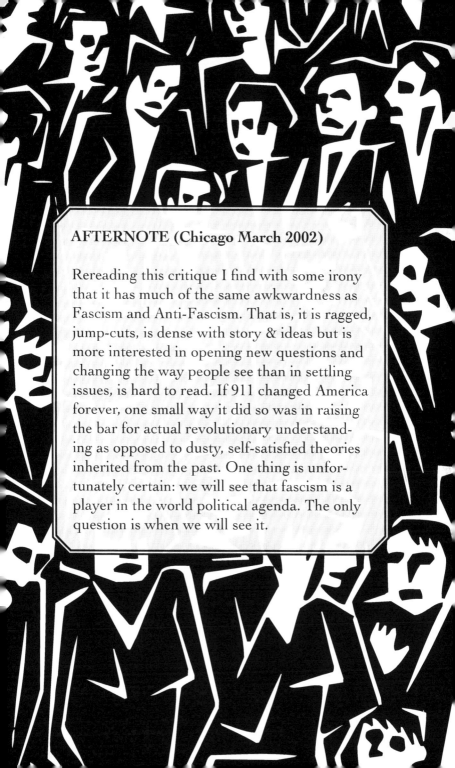

AFTERNOTE (Chicago March 2002)

Rereading this critique I find with some irony that it has much of the same awkwardness as Fascism and Anti-Fascism. That is, it is ragged, jump-cuts, is dense with story & ideas but is more interested in opening new questions and changing the way people see than in settling issues, is hard to read. If 911 changed America forever, one small way it did so was in raising the bar for actual revolutionary understanding as opposed to dusty, self-satisfied theories inherited from the past. One thing is unfortunately certain: we will see that fascism is a player in the world political agenda. The only question is when we will see it.

FOOTNOTES

Since I am not an academic, these footnotes were only grudgingly added after a reader of an advance draft protested that they needed footnotes to follow up on specific questions with further readings. Readers, more damned trouble than they're worth!

1. Benito Mussolini. *Opera Omnia*, Vol. I (Florence: La Fenice, 1951–63), p. 184. Quoted in Simonetta Falasca-Zamboni. *Fascist Spectacle. The Aesthetics of Power in Mussolini's Italy* (Berkeley & Los Angeles: University of California Press, 1997), p. 45. This book is particularly useful in understanding fascism because it approaches it from the vantage of art, of created mass culture.

2. These quotes were posted on fascist internet sites. Full texts in: M. Edwards. "Reports From the Homeland Front." In *ARA Research Bulletin #2* (Fall 2001, Chicago), p. 6

3. Atiba Shanna. *Sweeping The Notebooks 2: "Grains."* Informal document: n.p., n.d.

4. The basic facts about the Muslim Brotherhood as the original far right islamist political movement based in the lower middle classes are not controversial. R. Stephen Humphrey in his *Between Memory and Desire: the Middle East in a Troubled Age*, (University of California Press, 1999), describes the Brotherhood's founder and first Supreme Guide, Hasan al-Banna (a schoolteacher), as "a publicist and organizer of genius ... the real father of contemporary political Islam in the Sunni world." (see

pp. 190–193) Even if the Brotherhood had started as a purely spiritual group that later grew into the realm of politics, as it has claimed, we can still see those politics as inherent in that worldview (islam, like judaism and roman catholicism, has no separation between spiritual and secular). It could be easily argued that the Brotherhood protected itself with a screen of sincere religiosity, but that anti-colonial and anti-Western political impulses motivated it from the start. It was a semi-clandestine, highly disciplined clericalist political organization. Indeed, Humphrey writes that Hasan al-Banna's "dismay at the degree of foreign domination … drove him in 1928" to start the Brotherhood. Hasan al-Banna himself was killed in 1948 in reprisal for his secret terrorist unit's assassination of both the royal police commissioner and then the prime minister. Since then the Brotherhood took part in the overthrow of the Egyptian monarchy in 1952, and has attempted to seize state power in several countries, most notably Syria.

An interesting account of al-Banna was given by former Egyptian military ruler General Anwar el-Sadat, in his autobiography, *In Search of Identity* (Buccaneer Books, 1977). As a young officer in the Royal Egyptian Army in 1939, he had joined the Free Officers conspiracy to stage a coup against the Farouk monarchy and oust the British neo-colonial rulers. Sadat started giving his signals unit cautious political lectures. To his surprise, one of the unit's men asked if he, too, could address the soldiers. This man proved to be well-educated, explaining religious and other matters in a reasonable and informative manner. He was none other than Supreme Guide Hasan al-Banna himself. Sadat soon came to realize that the Brotherhood had an effective mass organization, and was "a power to be reckoned with." As for al-Banna's religious goals, Sadat comments (based on many private discussions) that "his activity had political ends." (pp. 22–23). Gen. Sadat obviously had his own axe to grind in this account, but given that the Brotherhood and the Free Officers Committee did make a secret alliance to overthrow the monarchy together his account is not so improbable. (The alliance and rivalry between the Brotherhood and the Officers is discussed in Humphrey as well as in William L. Cleveland's *A History of the Modern Middle East* [Westview Press, 1994]. See p. 289.)

The middle-class nature of the Muslim Brotherhood and similar early islamist clerical political groups is explored at more length by Michael Gilbert in his paper: "Popular Islam and the State in Contemporary Egypt." In Fred Halliday and Hamza Alavi. *State and Ideology in the Middle East and Pakistan* (Monthly Review Press, 1988).

5. Sara Lyall. "English Town Whispers Of a Taliban Connection." *New York Times*, February 3, 2002.

6. J. Sakai. "Aryan Politics & Fighting the WTO." In *My Enemy's Enemy: essays on globalization, fascism and the struggle against capitalism* (Montreal: Kersplebedeb, 2001).

7. Don Hamerquist. *Fascism in the U.S.? A Discussion Paper* (Chicago: Sojourner Truth Organization, 1976), p. 3.

8. For an interesting photograph of this slogan used in the context of Italian settler planned communities in colonial Ethiopia, see: Diane Ghirardo. *Building New Communities. New Deal America and Fascist Italy* (Princeton University Press, 1989), p. 103.

9. Robert Block. "In War on Terrorism, Sudan Struck a Blow By Fleecing bin Laden." *Wall Street Journal,* December 3, 2001.

10. J. Sakai. *Settlers. The Mythology of the White Proletariat From Mayflower to Modern* (Oakland/Montreal: PM Press/Kersplebedeb, 2014), 4th edition, pp. 143–151.

11. Hanna Batatu. "Syria's Muslim Brethren." In Halliday and Alavi. *State and Ideology in the Middle East and Pakistan* (Monthly Review Press, 1988).

12. *Internazionale Prese-Korrespondenz*, December 27, 1922. Quoted in Larry Ceplair. *Under the Shadow of War. Fascism, Anti-Fascism, and Marxists, 1918–1939* (Columbia University Press, 1987), p. 59.

13. Reproduced in Ian Kershaw. *Hitler. 1889–1936 Hubris* (W.W. Norton, 1999). Illustration no. 38.

14. Otto Friedrich. *Before The Deluge. A Portrait of Berlin in the 1920s* (New York: Fromm, 1986), p. 197.

15. Popular radical accounts of this relationship, such as Daniel Guerin's *Fascism and Big Business*, lean heavily on examples from after the 1930 elections and don't explain the significance of that. Some of the major capitalists, such as the Krupp interests, before then gave lump sums of money to right-wing figures that they trusted — General

Ludendorff is one example—who then doled it out between the different far right groups and veterans organizations. These indirect contributions were much sought after but not in any case strategic. Ian Kershaw, in his brilliant biography of Hitler, points out that in 1922–23: " … as would be the case later, the party's finances relied heavily upon members' subscriptions together with entrance-fees and collections at meetings." (p. 189) So we can throw out our received image of the Nazi Party as the subsidized and mercenary creation of the major capitalists. It was, in fact, popularly financed by its mass base.

It wasn't until after the Nazis took over the government in 1933 that Big Business backed them. In an extraordinary meeting on February 20, 1933, Hitler as Reich Chancellor met with the major industrialists for the first time. Arriving very late, Hitler lectured the businessmen on the need to subordinate economics to politics (they must have loved hearing that!), the fight to the death against communism, and other favorite themes for an hour and a half. He then accepted brief statements of support and quickly left the room. Herman Goering then demanded large financial contributions, and the assembled corporate barons agreed to give 3 million marks to the party. Kershaw sums it up as "the offering was less one of enthusiastic support than of political extortion." (pp. 447–448) At this point the left propaganda about fascism as the "puppets" of big business is laughable. Only the mis-estimation of fascism as a movement with its own class agenda had consequences that were not so amusing.

16. Otto Friedrich, pp. 283–284.

17. Kershaw. p. 334.

18. F.L. Carlson. *The Rise of Fascism* (University of California Press, 1967), Third edition, pp. 131–132.

19. Quoted in Carlson, p. 137.

20. Daniel Guerin. *The Brown Plague. Travels in Late Weimar and Early Nazi Germany* (Duke University Press, 1994), pp. 120–122.

21. Quoted in Carlson, p. 56

22. Quoted in S.J. Woolf. *European Fascism* (Vintage Books, 1969), pp. 43–44

23. R. Vacirca. Personal correspondence.

24. Quoted in Max Seydewitz. *Civil Life in Wartime Germany* (New York: Viking, 1945), p. 407. This is an interesting source because Seydewitz was a revolutionary socialist, who was an elected social-democratic member of the German legislature. He broke with the SPD in 1931 because of their failure to fight the fascists. A founder of the small SWP, he eventually escaped to exile in Sweden. His study is based on both the German wartime press and reports from the underground. As a side benefit we can see that the wartime Nazi press was essentially not any more censored about politics than our own ABC News or *Chicago Tribune*. Although, thanks to "democracy" we have learned a lot about Monica Lewinsky.

25. Seydewitz, p. 408.

26. A.J. Nicholls. "Germany." In Woolf, pp. 62–63. Although this quote is not sourced by Nicholls,

it probably comes from the former Nazi leader Hermann Rauschning, whose work is considered unreliable by most historians now because after he split with Hitler he wanted to paint him in the most radical light possible so as to discourage conservatives from supporting him. While his recollections of conversations with Hitler may not be literally accurate, they evoke better than most the violent inner essense of Hitler's fantastic worldview.

27. Adolf Hitler. *Mein Kampf* (Houghton Mifflin, 1971), pp. 373–378. Although Hitler's rep has required critics to always badrap his book, it's an exhilarating rip-roaring rant that easily roars past most left political writers. It is overly long, but so is the much duller *Das Kapital.* Supposedly a slimmed-down popular version, with the repetition and long detailed discussions about specifically German issues omitted, will be coming out next year.

28. Michael Burleigh and Wolfgang Wipperman. *The Racial State: Germany 1933–1945* (Cambridge and New York: Cambridge University Press, 1991), pp. 295–298.

29. Ibid.

30. Michael Burleigh. "… And Tomorrow The Whole World." In *History Today*, September 1990; Kershaw, p. 248.

31. Kershaw, p. 278.

32. Burleigh and Wipperman, op cit.

33. Richard Brookhiser. Review of "Theodore Rex." *New York Times Book Review*, December 9, 2001.

34. Kershaw, pp. 116–120.

35. Ibid.

36. Kershaw, p. 124.

37. Denis Mack Smith. *Mussolini* (New York: Alfred A. Knopf, 1982), p. 38.

38. Woolf, p. 46.

39. The account of Pakistani-Afghan events based on Ahmed Rashid. *Taliban: Militant Islam, Oil and Fundamentalism in Central Asia* (New Haven: Yale University Press, 2001).

40. *DAWN*, October 11, 2001 (Karachi).

41. i didn't footnote the entire Black Nation discussion because that would be basically phoney. Most of this story comes from discussions with participants, not from books. Other documents are legally tied up. Readers interested in State-gang relations might want to consult Edward Lee's *The Lumpenproletariat and Repression*, which appeared in a number of Puerto Rican MLN publications. On Farrakhan's complicity in the assassination of Malcolm X, this is obvious to all those who don't deny reality. Even former Farrakhan boosters like the cultural nationalists of Third World Press now admit he was guilty. For the George Lincoln Rockwell & the Nation of Islam quotes, see: *Chicago Reader*, April 11, 1986.

42. Commander Josh. *Into What World We Fall? Toward an anarchist perspective on 911 and its aftermath* (a Chicago discussion paper, October 2001).

*Antifas trash his pickup truck as
neofascist tries to escape at Battle of York.*

NOTES ON
THE BATTLE OF YORK

January 12, 2002, saw the first return to militant street action in the U.S. under this post-9/11 period of recession, repression and war. The scene was the small, blue-collar city of York, Pennsylvania, where ARA and other militants joined with local youth and clashed with a major white supremacist rally. While the numbers were only a small fraction of the crowds that swelled in Seattle to take on the WTO, we have a feeling that York could well be as much of a turning point for the movement as N30 was.

The neo-nazi rally was jointly sponsored by the World Church of the Creator and the National Alliance and supported by Aryan Nations, Eastern Hammerskins, WAR, the National Socialist Movement and other fascists. They chose York to take advantage of the climate following the arrest of the Democratic mayor for his role in a 1969 "race riot" there. The mayor, then a local cop, is accused of leading a white power rally (following the shooting of a police officer), urging attacks on the Black community, and actually arming white street gangs.

This first appeared as the Winter-Spring 2002 Editorial from Issue 3 of the *Anti-Racist Action Research Bulletin*.

The nazis hoped to stir up racial tensions in the city. What they got was determined resistance from the anti-fascist crowd who largely defeated the nazis in a hit-and-run battle over the course of the day. A dozen fascist vehicles were damaged and at least that many fascists pummelled. "It was a definite victory — though something short of decisive" for the anti-fascist movement, as a comrade's article describes it.

But victories are easily reversed if we don't take careful measure of such "turning points," deal honestly and constructively with our weaknesses, and make real preparations for operating on a higher level. Here are a few notes towards that effort.

THE FASCIST RESPONSE

Despite the usual huff and puff from Matt Hale and other fascists who claimed a victory, the bulk of the fascist movement understood York was a defeat for them. This was one of their largest mobilizations in years and many had to flee in humiliation. Some fascist leaders claimed a victory based on turnout and media attention alone, though even they must understand that it hurts their organizing to lose confrontations like this.

They are not happy with this outcome, and some form of retaliation is headed our way. Aryan Nations is howling for blood and there is more talk among the fascists of gathering intel on us and targeting

ARA's perceived leadership. Surely the National Alliance knows that it needs to win some decisive victories against us if they want their street actions to gain strength. Some fascists are probably looking to deliver large numbers of us (or at least our core activists) into the hands of the state. The post-York discussion among fascists focused on how they can be more prepared for confrontation in the future with weapons, security, communication and tactics. They will be much more careful in future planning and we should be cautious of set-ups.

One thing needs to be emphasized again. We are not bulletproof. The fascists are very heavily armed, and it would be foolish to think that they will never use them. In York, the nazis actually pulled out pieces on three separate occasions when they were coming under attack. If one of us would've been shot it obviously would've changed everything. Some fascists may actually have in mind to stage another Greensboro (when armed Klansmen drove up on and shot militant anti-racists), hoping to achieve the street-level victory they need over us. We can be sure that some of the fascists are informants, and just like Greensboro, informants have state protection and so feel like they can literally get away with murder. Our security and self-defense capabilities have to match the level of struggle we are engaged in.

York was a unified action that pulled together many (often opposed) fascist groups, partly due to the influence the National Alliance has gained over the movement. But York also opened up divisions among the fascists. Many were disgusted with the way Matt Hale was whisked away under "ZOG" protection while the rank and file took it on the chin. We need to understand these divisions and find methods of attack to further exacerbate them.

STATE REPRESSION

An escalating conflict between white supremacists and radical anti-fascists will not go unnoticed by the state. In fact, federal police agencies have been following developments in our movement—and in the fascist movement—for some time. This project has undoubtedly increased with the emergence of the militant anti-capitalist wing of the anti-globalization movement and was probably given a blank check in the wake of the Sepember 11th attacks.

The main thrust of the authorities' repressive efforts towards anti-fascism will be to isolate militants from our potential mass base, co-opt and contain whatever section of the movement it can, and promote a less troublesome, more loyal brand of anti-fascism. They will work towards this through the media, through pressure from liberal "anti-racists," and through infiltrators in our own ranks who will attempt to steer us in the direction the state wishes.

The Anti-Defamation League (ADL) and Southern Poverty Law Center (SPLC) are already playing leading roles in this tack. The line they are broadcasting, with the eager help of the mainstream media, is that there is essentially no difference between ARA and the nazis—in their characterization, we are both irrational, violent extremists.

If this kind of disinformation is allowed to take hold in the public consciousness, it will be much easier for moderates to argue that our radicalism is preventing us from reaching real people. A lack of popular sympathy will allow any harder forms of repression (brutality, imprisonment, dismantling of radical structures) deemed necessary or advantageous to go more smoothly.

Our task is to be vigilant against these undermining attacks, to get our undiluted politics out there, and to continue to develop a mass base of support and participation for revolutionary anti-fascist ideas and action.

POPULAR STRUGGLE

The exceptional thing about the Battle of York was not the successful physical confrontation of nazis (we've done that before), it was the active participation of large numbers of local Black, Puerto Rican and white youth (and some older folks as well). This is what transformed the action from a clash of politicos into an insurgent community defense.

ARA's pledge of "we go where they go" ends up taking us places where the rest of the Left does not tread. We need to reach out into all communities where we're active, attempt to set up ARA groups where we can, and give concrete solidarity to other struggles: against police brutality, for women's and queer freedom, in neighborhoods and workplaces, against poverty, etc. It is important that we follow up actions in York with community outreach and use these struggles to build an even stronger movement.

We also need to make effective use of the media (including the corporate mass-media) to counter the ADL/SPLC spin, remaining extremely wary of media attempts to turn us into spectacle, or create "leaders" over the movement.

It is crucial we continue to develop an anti-fascist culture, truly liberatory and in sharp contrast to the fascists' racist, patriarchal, nationalistic and hierarchical vibe. It will be by those standards that people will ultimately measure our differences with the fascists, not simply by written programs or by military victories.

The Battle of York offers up many lessons and insights into the struggle ahead. Let's take full advantage of them.

THE ANTI-RACIST ACTION NETWORK'S FOUR POINTS OF UNITY

1) WE GO WHERE THEY GO: Whenever fascists are organizing or active in public, we're there. We don't believe in ignoring them or staying away from them. Never let the nazis have the street!

2) WE DON'T RELY ON THE COPS OR THE COURTS TO DO OUR WORK: This doesn't mean we don't ever go to court. But we must rely on ourselves to protect ourselves and stop the fascists.

3) NON-SECTARIAN DEFENSE OF OTHER ANTI-FASCISTS: In ARA, we have lots of groups and individuals. We don't agree about everything, and we have the right to differ openly. But in this movement an attack on one is an attack on us all. We stand behind each other.

4) WE SUPPORT ABORTION RIGHTS AND REPRODUCTIVE FREEDOM.

ARA intends to do the hard work necessary to build a broad, strong movement against racism, sexism, anti-Semitism, homophobia, discrimination against the disabled, the oldest, the youngest, and the most oppressed people. **WE INTEND TO WIN!**

Red Pioneers (Communist Party Youth group) demonstrating against fascism—Berlin, 1932.

REVOLUTIONARY ANTI-FASCISM: SOME STRATEGIC QUESTIONS

by Mark Salotte

There is a general consensus in the movement—and in the broader society today—that N30 in Seattle was the announcement of a new phase of struggle for the left. One in which decentralization, anarchist and anti-authoritarian ideas, and international "horizontally-linked" struggles would play a central role as common reference points for all involved. While the "post-Seattle landscape" to most observers, from critics to police and the state to movement tacticians, refers primarily to street tactics, these organizational and philosophical changes have a comparable impact on all of us. Suddenly people are speaking our language, some of whom we don't see eye to eye with on just about anything, and those of us on the anti-racist, anti-capitalist, anti-authoritarian "left" have been so stunned we haven't figured out how to respond quite yet.

In the days of the Tower of Babel, a movement was effectively broken up by confusing the people's tongues so they spoke different languages and could no longer understand each other. What's happening

Nazis wave German battle-flag at York confrontation.

today is the process in reverse: now everyone speaks the same language and means completely different things by it. When our enemies are using the same terms to describe themselves as we do, how do we explain to people what we stand for and how that's different from what our enemies offer?

"Libertarian communism" and "anarchist communism" look to a movement where class war and working-class resistance can break the boundaries of nationalist bigotry, while "libertarian socialism" looks to stir up nationalist and ethnic rivalries to crush class solidarity. Some anarchists identify as "anti-imperialists" and, with varying degrees of integrity, take inspiration from and offer support to leftist and anti-authoritarian currents within black, Puerto Rican, and other nationalist struggles. While on the other hand, there are "national anarchists" who look for the right-wing elements in those same nationalist struggles, and ally with those elements while organizing for a right-wing white nationalist movement. It gets hard for a lot of people to tell friend from foe these days.

Puzzling these questions out is essential if we hope to move forward in any way. The defining line as we see it is the relationship between class struggle and nationalism. While traditional terms like "left" and "right" may not carry the same meaning to activists today they once did—in some cases they barely have any meaning left at all—we're not ready to follow the lead of many in the "primitivist" and "deep ecology" scenes in abandoning them altogether. The vital contribution of anti-fascism to the movement today lies in analyzing all the forces, separating "friend" from "foe," and suggesting directions in organizing and strategic alliances that would strengthen the anti-racist and anti-nationalist tendencies of the movement and isolate the reactionary tendencies.

An interesting historical document to compare against our situation today is an essay by Wilhelm Reich called *What is Class Consciousness?*—written from exile a year after the Nazi Party came to power in Germany. Reich brings up many interesting questions regarding the failure of the left to effectively oppose the politics of National Socialism. He begins by analyzing the current situation:

> "The Sex-Pol working community believes that there are three main possibilities. First, there is the possibility of an unpredictable uprising in Germany in the near future. Since none of the existing organizations is even remotely prepared

for such an eventuality, none of them could control such a movement or lead it consciously to a conclusion. This possibility, however, is the least likely. Should it happen, the situation would be chaotic and the outcome extremely uncertain, but it would nevertheless be the best solution, and we should support it and promote it from the very start. Second, the working-class movement may need a few years before it rallies once more in terms of theory and organization. It will then form an integrated movement under good, highly trained, and determined leadership, will struggle for power in Germany, and will seize it within, say, the next two decades. This prospect is the most probable, but it requires energetic, unswerving and tireless preparation beginning today. Third, the last major possibility is that the

rallying of the working-class movement under new, good and reliable leadership will not occur quickly enough or will fail to occur altogether; that international fascism will establish itself and consolidate its positions everywhere, especially by reason of its immanent skill in attracting children and youth; that it will acquire a permanent mass base, and will be helped by economic conjunctures, however marginal. In such a case the socialist movement must reckon with a long—a very long—period of economic, cultural, and political barbarism lasting many decades. Its task then will be to prove that it was not mistaken in principle and that, in the last analysis, it was right after all. This prospect reveals the full extent of the responsibility we bear.

"We propose, so far as conditions permit, to allow for the first possibility; to make the second the real target of our work, because it is the more likely one, and to concentrate all our efforts on bringing it about while doing everything within human possibility to avoid the third."

As we know, the left failed on all three of these counts. No real spontaneous uprising ever threatened the Nazis. Conservative Catholic and monarchist groups tried a few half-hearted protests, but for the most part the only people who even resisted the Nazis were working-class street gangs who were very early on repressed and killed. The communist movement never managed to regroup in any serious way. And even after Nazism was defeated militarily by outside imperialism, it was still rooted in mass culture a lot deeper than socialism. It took another generation for the left to pull itself together as something more than a middle-class academic fashion. And yet, still, it seems that Reich was basically right in his whole analysis. Not that he could have led the rebirth of the anti-fascist movement, but that in order to rebuild itself, the movement would have had to be thinking in the way he was trying to lay out.

This is particularly interesting to us today. From a revolutionary anti-fascist perspective, we can similarly break down the possibilities presented to us by the current situation. First, the "anti-capitalist" movement could continue to grow, overcoming the inevitable setbacks and outflanking the state's attempt to contain us. In such a scenario, autonomous zones created by insurrections or long-term organizing projects would turn into liberated spaces. The movement could manage to link up with ghetto, barrio, and neighborhood uprisings and organizing in cities and with workplace struggles everywhere, manage to build alliances with rebel militias in rural areas, and get to a point where our autonomy seriously threatens the stability of the state. This, I think should be obvious, is a very remote possibility. The necessary links are just barely starting to be made and are hampered by a lot of arrogance within the movement. The movement's class politics may be much too weak to really attract the allies we need, and our tacticians may not have the experience necessary to out-think the professional police just yet.

A more likely possibility is that in time, we may find ourselves temporarily stalled or contained by the state. If our assessment of the determination and interest that people have been showing in radical politics lately is accurate, it seems very unlikely that anytime soon our movement will be completely defeated or even forced back to pre-Seattle levels of activity. But it's easy to see a situation where the state will be able to prevent us from mounting the kind of large actions that have been the public face of anarchism over the past few years. And at the same time that the state's political forces are working to contain us organizationally and militarily, its conservative and liberal supporters are also trying to defeat us politically by using mass propaganda to push nationalist, xenophobic, religious, and racially inflammatory attitudes among the American population. In such a situation, the growing neo-fascist movement, which has enjoyed extremely low levels of political repression for the past few decades, will find itself in a position to pick up the initiative we've built with our organizing. Even the possibility of this situation — and we see it as being quite possible — demands that anti-fascist work be made a priority today. This work is important to both track and prevent the growth of organizations that could play this role down the road. It can also, in a more general way, counter the social attitudes — promoted today by almost every wing of the government, the church, and the media — that provide fertile ground for fascist organizing.

A third possibility involves the state managing to contain both the anti-capitalist left and the fascist right, and move towards an ultra-centralized authoritarian fascism on its own. This is the possibility that the militias et al have been warning about for years, although many of them haven't been able to read the signs that it has become a real potential. The Bush coup last election, the conveniently-timed war on terrorism, and basically everything that's happened since show that this is on the agenda of at least some elements in the ruling class. Who needs some outdated racial theories imported from Europe when we have good old American jingoism, conservative christianity, and a multi-culturalist gloss to hold together mass support for a major change in the government? The task of the left in this case is to consistently talk to people on the street, and point out the obvious contradictions between these elements of the state's "official religion." For example, a little while ago there was a bit of a scandal when one of Bush's Secret Service men, an Arab-American, was forced off a plane and questioned as a suspected terrorist.

Scenes from the Battle of York.

This highlighted the contradiction between the classic xenophobia being pushed to support the war effort and the illusion essential for continued capitalist market growth that America is a color-blind "land of opportunity." Events like these usually get buried in the media pretty quickly, but in the present situation, they're bound to happen regularly, and they always leave at least a little opening for us to point to and expose the state's plots behind the scenes.

The anti-fascist movement right now has a strong momentum and a clear direction, at a time when much of the revolutionary anarchist scene is regrouping its forces and questioning its politics. For that reason, groups who identify with the revolutionary anti-fascist tradition have an opportunity—and an obligation—to lead by example.

The January 12th mobilization in York was a turning point for us. It was a definite victory—although something short of decisive—in the streets, but more importantly, it gave us back the upper hand politically. For some time now, the white power movement has been concentrating its forces in the mid-Atlantic area; we correctly recognized that situation, picked a point to engage them at, and stopped their momentum in its tracks. York was the first—and far from the last—street showdown in this part of the country between the neo-nazis and us. But the showing we had was strong enough to guarantee that the streets will be ours unless the nazis win a major propaganda victory over us that can change the balance of forces. So therefore, the terrain this war will be fought on will be the world of public opinion where we already have some groundwork laid, rather than the empty symbolism of street demonstrations that the Nazis thrive on. This in and of itself is a huge victory for us.

So how do we move forward? Well, we should recognize that our politics are a few steps ahead of the fascists right now. While we still need to be on the ground stopping their organizing, we also have a chance to move ahead and actually start organizing and offering solutions where the fascists are still trying to sell images. This will mean talking with people on the ground, organizing public events and building ongoing people's institutions where that's possible.

Antifascist Resources

This is a partial list of some antifascist organizations active in the United States in early 2017, at the time that this book is going to press. A more complete list is being assembled and will be made available here:

THREEWAYFIGHT.BLOGSPOT.COM/P/ ANTIFASCIST-RESOURCES_20.HTML

Anti-Fascist News
https://antifascistnews.net

Anti-Racist Action Los Angeles / People Against Racist Terror
P.O. Box 1055
Culver City, CA 90232

www.antiracist.org

First of May Anarchist Alliance
http://m1aa.org/

International Anti-Fascist Defence Fund
intlantifadefence.wordpress.com

It's Going Down
https://itsgoingdown.org/

NYC Antifa
https://nycantifa.wordpress.com

One People Project
P.O. Box 42817
Philadelphia, PA 19101

www.onepeoplesproject.com
www.idavox.com/

Philly Antifa
https://phillyantifa.noblogs.org

Political Research Associates
1310 Broadway, Suite 201
Somerville, MA 02144

www.politicalresearch.org

Rose City Antifa
www.rosecityantifa.org

Three Way Fight
www.threewayfight.blogspot.com

Torch Antifascist Network
www.torchantifa.org

Twin Cities General Defense Committee
https://twincitiesgdc.org/
https://www.facebook.com/TC.GDC
https://twitter.com/tcgdc

GLOBAL ANTIFA PRISONER LIST, AND INFORMATION ABOUT THE ANNUAL JULY 25TH INTERNATIONAL DAY OF SOLIDARITY WITH ANTIFASCIST PRISONERS
HTTPS://NYCANTIFA.WORDPRESS.COM/GLOBAL-ANTIFA-PRISONER-LIST

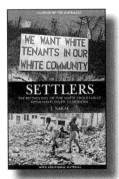

Settlers: The Mythology of the White Proletariat from Mayflower to Modern

J. Sakai • 978-1-62963-037-3
456 pages • $20.00

J. Sakai shows how the United States is a country built on the theft of Indigenous lands and Afrikan labor, on the robbery of the northern third of Mexico, the colonization of Puerto Rico, and the expropriation of the Asian working class, with each of these crimes being accompanied by violence. In fact, America's white citizenry have never supported themselves but have always resorted to exploitation and theft, culminating in acts of genocide to maintain their culture and way of life. This movement classic lays it all out, taking us through this painful but important history.

Night-Vision: Illuminating War and Class on the Neo-Colonial Terrain

Butch Lee & Red Rover • 978-1-894946-88-9
240 pages • $16.95

A foundational analysis of post-modern capitalism, the decline of u.s. hegemony, and the need for a revolutionary movement of the oppressed to overthrow it all. In the words of bell hooks: "Night-Vision was so compelling to me because it has a spirit of militancy which reformist feminism tries to kill because militant feminism is seen as a threat to the liberal bourgeois feminism that just wants to be equal with men. It has that raw, unmediated truth-telling which I think we are going to need in order to deal with the fascism that's upon us."

Meditations on Frantz Fanon's Wretched of the Earth: New Afrikan Revolutionary Writings

James Yaki Sayles • 978-1-894946-32-2
399 pages • $20.00

One of those who eagerly picked up Fanon in the '60s, who carried out armed expropriations and violence against white settlers, Sayles reveals how, behind the image of Fanon as race thinker, there is an underlying reality of antiracist communist thought.

Basic Politics of Movement Security: "A Talk on Security" by J. Sakai & "G20 Repression & Infiltration in Toronto: An Interview with Mandy Hiscocks"

J. Sakai & Mandy Hiscocks • 9781894946520
72 pages • $7.00

There are many books and articles reporting state repression, but not on that subject's more intimate relative, movement security. It is general practice to only pass along knowledge about movement security privately, in closed group lectures or by personal word-of-mouth. Adding to the confusion, the handful of available left security texts are usually about underground or illegal groups, not the far larger public movements that work on a more or less legal level. Based on their own personal experiences on this terrain, these two "live" discussions by radical activists provide a partial remedy to this situation.

CTRL-ALT-DELETE:
An Antifascist Report on the Alternative Right

CTRL-ALT-DELETE

Ctrl-Alt-Delete:
An Antifascist Report
on the Alternative Right
Matthew N. Lyons

The Rich Kids of Fascism
It's Going Down

Black Genocide and the Alt-Right
K. Kersplebedeb

Notes on Trump
Bromma

978-1894946858 ✦ 122 PAGES ✦ $10.00

Addressing the origins and rise of the so-called "alt-right," the fascistic movement that grabbed headlines in the months leading up to the 2016 election of Donald Trump as president of the United States.

Matthew Lyons and It's Going Down examine different facets of the alt-right, its constituent parts and beliefs at the present time, its class base, strengths and weaknesses, as well as observations about how its future relationship with the Trump administration may play out. K. Kersplebedeb breaks down the impetus towards genocide in the alt-right's racist rhetoric, while an additional text, by Bromma, provides a useful series of observations about the broader political and economic context that is fueling not only the alt-right, but all manner of other reactionary developments as well.

The alt-right in one expression of the reactionary moment our movements have been plunged into in 2017. We must oppose them, all the while preparing to oppose what might come next.

INSURGENT SUPREMACISTS:
The U.S. Far Right's Challenge to State and Empire

INSURGENT SUPREMACISTS

The U.S. Far Right's
Challenge to State and Empire

Matthew N. Lyons

TO BE RELEASED BY KERSPLEBEDEB
AND PM PRESS IN 2018

A major study of movements that strive to overthrow the U.S. government, that often claim to be anti-imperialist and sometimes even anti-capitalist ... and which also consciously promote inequality, hierarchy, and domination, generally along explicitly racist, sexist, and homophobic lines. Revolutionaries of the far right: insurgent supremacists.

In this book, Matthew N. Lyons takes readers on a tour of neonazis and Christian theocrats, by way of the Patriot Movement, the Larouchites, and the Alt-Right. Supplementing this, thematic sections expore specific dimensions of far right politics, regarding gender, decentralism, and anti-imperialism.

Finally, intervening directly in debates within left and anti-fascist movements, Lyons examines both the widespread use and abuse of the term "fascism," and the relationship between federal security forces and the paramilitary right.

Both for its analysis and as a guide to our opponents, *Insurgent Supremacists* promises to be a powerful tool in organizing to resist the forces at the cutting edge of reaction today.

KER
SPL
EBE
DEB

Since 1998 Kersplebedeb has been an important source of radical literature and agit prop materials.

The project has a non-exclusive focus on anti-patriarchal and anti-imperialist politics, framed within an anticapitalist perspective. A special priority is given to writings regarding armed struggle in the metropole, and the continuing struggles of political prisoners and prisoners of war.

The Kersplebedeb website presents historical and contemporary writings by revolutionary thinkers from the anarchist and communist traditions.

Kersplebedeb can be contacted at:

Kersplebedeb
CP 63560
CCCP Van Horne
Montreal, Quebec
Canada
H3W 3H8

email: info@kersplebedeb.com
web: www.kersplebedeb.com
  www.leftwingbooks.net

Kersplebedeb

Made in the USA
Coppell, TX
22 November 2024